D0835233

THE
LEADERSHIP
DYNAMIC

THE
LEADERSHIP DYNAMIC

A Biblical Model for Raising Effective Leaders

HARRY L. REEDER III
with ROD GRAGG

CROSSWAY BOOKS

WHEATON, ILLINOIS

The Leadership Dynamic: A Biblical Model for Raising Effective Leaders
Copyright © 2008 by Harry L. Reeder III
Published by Crossway Books
    a publishing ministry of Good News Publishers
    1300 Crescent Street
    Wheaton, Illinois 60187

Interior design and typesetting: Lakeside Design Plus
Cover design: Amy Bristow
Cover photo: Getty Images

First printing 2008
Printed in the United States of America

Unless otherwise indicated, Scripture quotations are from *The Holy Bible, English Standard Version*®, copyright © 2001 by Crossway Bibles, a publishing ministry of Good News Publishers. Used by permission. All rights reserved.

Scripture quotations marked KJV are from the *King James Version* of the Bible.

Scripture quotations marked NASB are from *The New American Standard Bible*®. Copyright © The Lockman Foundation 1960, 1962, 1963, 1968, 1971, 1972, 1973, 1975, 1977, 1995. Used by permission.

Scripture references marked NIV are from *The Holy Bible: New International Version*®. Copyright © 1973, 1978, 1984 by International Bible Society. Used by permission of Zondervan Publishing House. All rights reserved.

The "NIV" and "New International Version" trademarks are registered in the United States Patent and Trademark Office by International Bible Society. Use of either trademark requires the permission of International Bible Society.

All emphases in Scripture quotations have been added by the author.

Trade Paperback ISBN: 978-1-58134-943-6
PDF ISBN: 978-1-4335-0438-9
Mobipocket ISBN: 978-1-4335-0439-6

Library of Congress Cataloging-in-Publication Data
Reeder, Harry L., 1948–
    The leadership dynamic : a biblical model for raising effective leaders / Harry L. Reeder III, with Rod Gragg.
        p. cm.
    Includes bibliographical references and index.
    ISBN 978-1-58134-943-6 (tpb)
    1. Leadership—Biblical teaching. I. Gragg, Rod. II. Title.

BS680.L4R44 2008
261—dc22
                                                                  2008011612

VP   16   15   14   13   12   11   10   09   08
              9   8   7   6   5   4   3   2   1

CONTENTS

PREFACE

I f I were to begin my ministry as a pastor tomorrow knowing what I know today, there is one commitment that I would elevate in terms of priority and attention. That one commitment is leadership. Specifically I would commit myself to defining with greater clarity the biblical concept of a leader. Then, I would commit to investing more time and focus in developing leaders committed to that biblical concept of leadership. Finally, I would seek ways to deploy them not only in the church and their families but into every honorable sphere of influence in our culture. If I could begin my ministry again, I would certainly seek to be more consistent in intercessory prayer and more effective as an expositional preacher of the Word, and in fact, I do not know of a single area of ministry priority where I would not desire to grow in faithfulness and competency. But, the one thing that I would elevate on my priority list is what I am calling in this book Three-*D* leadership: defining, developing, and deploying Christian leaders who are capable of transforming society through their Christ-centered and gospel-driven lifestyle and leadership and who will intentionally multiply themselves.

I believe this is a biblical strategy that our Lord clearly prioritized in his three-year public ministry. It is also clear that the great movements of history in general and the movements of God's kingdom in particular have always been driven by multiplication leadership. God's Word is replete with a multitude of such examples. Consistently, whenever God decided to do something he called grace-driven, character-based leaders to initiate his mission, and they in turn unfailingly multiplied themselves through other leaders.

Furthermore, this is an unbelievable moment of opportunity throughout the cultures of this world. The moment has been created by a vacuum of good leadership and a simultaneous phenomenon of cynicism and discouragement concerning leadership, which the present leaders and concepts of leadership dominating our world today have produced.

The burden of this book is simple. Let's return to the mandate, the mission, and the biblical model of Christian leadership and intentional leadership multiplication. If we succeed, then the church again will become a leadership factory and distribution center. Join me as we anticipate God's answers from his Word as to how our God would do this through us to extend his glorious kingdom, redeem lost men and women, and transform the landscape of our world.

I would like to thank my Lord and Savior for allowing me to know him savingly and personally and to serve him vocationally. In that relationship, this entire vision for the leadership dynamic has been birthed throughout many years. May our Lord be pleased to bless this effort as I gratefully thank him for the enormous blessing of serving the Triune God and his church and proclaiming the gospel of his kingdom.

I would like to thank Crossway Books, Allan Fisher and his entire team, and Rod Gragg who significantly assisted in the writing of the manuscript. To Briarwood Presbyterian Church I am grateful for the privilege to serve the Lord with you and for the encouragement of not only our members but also our elders, deacons, and pastoral staff—without whom this effort could never have been accomplished.

I owe an enormous thanks to the diligent labor and untiring efforts of my ministry assistant, Marie Gathings, the consultation of Tara Miller, and the preliminary editing of Linda Waugh. To my family, I am forever grateful. My sisters Vickie, Amy, and Beth along with their husbands have been a constant encouragement and prayer support. I praise the Lord for my children Jennifer, Ike, and Abigail, her husband Ryan, and our grandchildren, Brianna, CJ, Mack, Matthias, and Taylor. To Cindy, my precious wife, who is my ever present inspiration, encouragement, and counselor, I wish to especially dedicate this effort. Perhaps more than anyone else she manifests the biblical concept of servant leadership. I also wish to acknowledge my dad and mom who now reside in the presence of their Lord and who taught in precept and practice much of what I later learned to know as Christian leadership.

In conclusion, to all of the pastors who desire to serve the Lord, proclaim the gospel, equip the saints, fulfill the Great Commission, and see a gospel-driven transformation of their church, their community, and their world, this book is especially dedicated. May our Lord bless you as you seek to first be faithful, by God's grace effective, and for God's glory influential for the preeminence of Christ. May our Lord allow you to lead his church, founded upon the ministry of prayer and the Word, to be a leadership factory and distribution center and together may we hear again, "These men who have turned the world upside down have come here also" (Acts 17:6).

1

GOD'S MODEL FOR LEADERSHIP

"These men who have turned the world upside down
have come here also."

W hy do we do it?
Why do Christians want to learn leadership from the world's models when we know that "worldly wisdom" inevitably conflicts with the Word of God and brings chaos and despair? Genuine, effective leadership must be learned from God's Word, developed through disciple making, nurtured in God's church, and then transported into the world. When this happens, we can anticipate a consistent reproduction of multiplication leaders who have been transformed by biblical leadership. It's God's chain reaction. A transformed leader produces more transformed leaders—leaders who have been mentored within the church, then sent out to impact the world. By God's grace they will become change agents, and the process will continually repeat itself just as God intended. By faithfully applying the model of leadership revealed in the Word of God, the church can

again turn the world upside down. At the moment, however, we face a cultural meltdown.

The Contemporary American Model

The American church is standing at the brink of a self-inflicted death spiral accelerated by worldly leadership. God's people are the "salt" and "light" of surrounding culture, so when the church begins its free fall, all of American culture will soon follow. What's the poisonous elixir that the contemporary American church seems so determined to consume? The answer: the leadership model now practiced and promoted in the boardrooms of American big business. What? Is traditional American capitalism wrong? Unbiblical? Dangerous? The answer is no—*traditional* capitalism is not the problem. The leadership model that is infecting the church today—with disastrous results—is a product of *contemporary* capitalism, which is a greed-based, wealth-consuming mutation that has replaced the historically Christian-influenced system of capitalism that created the wealth upon which our nation thrived and blessed the world. Today's self-promoting, infected corporate leadership is a deadly potion that countless churches are drinking as they thoughtlessly imbibe the contemporary corporate leadership models of the day.

Christian-influenced capitalism was put to work immediately on American soil, and helped to shape our nation in a powerfully positive manner. The fresh influence of the Protestant Reformation spilled into America's English colonies, forging American law and culture based on the Judeo-Christian worldview. Our nation was founded on that biblical consensus and flourished with it as it kept improving ethically and practically—until the American worldview completed its shift to secular humanism in the late twentieth century. The biblical worldview holds that God is the authority over all things, and that pleasing him should be the foundation of every endeavor. Secular humanism proclaims that man, not God, is the final authority and that everything exists for personal pleasure and affluence.

Historically, the influence of Christianity on American capitalism produced a huge and generally prosperous middle class that provided economic and cultural stability for the nation. Influenced by Christian leadership, traditional American capitalism increasingly promoted a lofty goal—that corporate success is not the *consumption* of wealth but the *creation* of it. It was not greed that was good, but doing good was good. The foundational ethic of traditional American capitalism—as influenced by Christianity—was not simply to "do what is good for business" but to "make it your business to do good." Through the ages, Christian-influenced traditional American capitalism kept producing more and more extraordinary business leaders who also excelled as philanthropists by creating jobs, investing in the community, assisting the needy, providing meaningful public service, supporting the church, and in other ways making communities better. Surely there were a number of greedy business leaders, but they were marginalized, and certainly they were not celebrated as they are today. Historically in America, God's people—the church—influenced American capitalism to practice a biblical model of servant leadership. Today, contemporary capitalism is influencing the church to practice a model of self-absorbed leadership. Yesterday the church produced effective servant leaders for the world of business. Today the world produces self-promoting leaders who are infecting the church.

Just as the biblical worldview affected all aspects of culture for most of American history, secular humanism today influences our bedrock institutions: law, government, education, healthcare, media, the arts, and the business community. This repackaged paganism embraced by contemporary American capitalism has rejected the influence of biblical truth in order to embrace a self-absorbed leadership model that promotes self-worship. Yet—alarmingly—much of the American church today is either thoughtlessly or pragmatically employing a humanistic model of contemporary capitalistic leadership. And the model is not only unbiblical but its ability to permeate the culture is ultimately destructive.

Recently the evidence of this downward spiral in contemporary corporate America was manifested by entire corporations faltering and closing, not because of problems on the ground floors but because of moral failures in the executive offices of leaders acting on their personal and greedy quest for wealth and power. This produced a staggering loss of jobs, obliteration of countless individual retirement packages, untold numbers of divorces and wrecked families, widespread erosion of respect for the business community, the demise of the dreams of many, and a general loss of respect for the American free-enterprise system. Business leadership today is too often not about *leadership* but about the *leader*—his or her power, portfolio, and profits. The lack of biblically based leadership in American culture has left our society reeling like a boxer on the ropes after a knockout punch.

Modern corporate leadership is rooted in self-absorbed concepts of success, ego-driven desires for power, and what is now a socially approved expression of greed that a century ago would have been decried as evil. This self-worshiping, man-centered model of leadership is promoted anew every semester through collegiate MBA programs. American educational institutions are the front line of the culture war as the typical university is militantly intolerant to any idea that would propose ethical absolutes in any degree program. Few university MBA programs today instruct future business leaders in the traditional, biblically based ethic of sacrificial servant leadership. In fact, only a pitiful few MBA programs retain a course on business ethics. Traditional American capitalism, along with the Judeo-Christian worldview on which it was based, is fiercely rejected at today's typical university. What's being taught instead? Pragmatism rules. The end justifies the means. Ethics are not absolutes to be obeyed, but obstacles to be overcome. And now, voraciously, this humanistic, greed-driven model of leadership is being adopted and absorbed by churches throughout our nation. Yet greed destroys. This popular new model of corporate leadership will eventually destroy the American church if unchecked and if continued as the primary source of leadership models and/or leaders themselves. What can be done to stop this deadly plunge into a black hole of destructive leadership? Can the church profit from certain aspects of how to do business from corporate America? Certainly. But the church is not a business. We do not produce a product to be bought; members are not customers. Pastors are not CEOs, and leaders are not a board of directors. Secondly, the church certainly cannot imbibe the diving dynamics of death from today's greed-based and self-promoting culture-destroying leadership found in many executive offices of America's business world. The church must escape the swamp of greed-driven leadership prevalent in contemporary corporate America and ascend the high ground of gospel-driven leadership described in God's Word.

The Biblical Model

Regaining lost ground won't be easy, but the solution is simple: the church must follow the Bible's model for *defining, developing,* and *deploying* leaders while simultaneously rejecting the world's leadership models and standards. Simply put, the American church must *define* leadership and then *develop* and *deploy* leaders who can transform the world for Jesus Christ. How do we do it? Obviously, raising leaders for such a time as this will require more than a couple of officer training classes or a few sermons on Christian leadership. The Christian church must become a leadership factory and distribution center for the world, and by the grace of God, it can—if we return to both the biblical definition of leadership and the biblical method of producing leaders for the church and the world.

The first step for the church, from denominational headquarters to pastors facing the pews each Sunday, is to clearly define the biblical model of leadership. Initially that will require turning away from the unbiblical models of leadership that have infiltrated denominational literature, popular leadership manuals, and local church leadership training classes. Take a close and honest look at what is passing for leadership training in many modern American churches. First, promoting personal self-esteem is seen by many as the key call of the church. How wrong is that? A self-centered life is exactly the opposite of Christ's call to a God-centered life and the essence of Christian leadership, which demands a servant heart and sacrificial life. Today's focus on self-esteem is profiled not by Scripture, but by the current preoccupation with narcissism. It is "all about me," therefore Christianity is being repackaged and redefined as a self-absorbed system of self-esteem. Sadly, the love of self is deeply embedded in contemporary American culture, including the church, because we have embedded the leaders of the culture into the leadership of the church. We now face a generation of church members—and leaders—who are encouraged to constantly ask themselves, how good do *I* feel about myself? how good do *you* make me feel about myself? how good does the *church* make me feel about myself? and, by the way, how good does *Jesus* make me feel about myself? The church has succumbed to the secular cultural pressure of promoting self-esteem, instead of sharing the gospel call to die to self through a God-centered life, and if you miss the gospel-driven Christian life, it is impossible to produce Christian leaders.

This counterfeit leadership training also encourages absorption with physical and material prosperity that easily becomes idolatry. The salvation offered by Jesus Christ is thus perverted into a "prosperity gospel," defined by self-centered materialism that assures true believers that they will become healthy and wealthy if they only "confess it and possess it," "name it and claim it," or "believe it and receive it"! Where did this perversion of Christianity come from? Certainly not the Bible. The Word of God firmly promises that our God "will supply all your needs" (Phil. 4:19, NASB) in Christ Jesus and, "I can do all things through him [Christ] who strengthens me." (Phil. 4:13, NASB). Why? So that I can be "poured out as a drink offering" (Phil. 2:17) and embrace the call of our Savior—"for me to live is Christ" (Phil. 1:21) and "it is no longer I who live, but Christ who lives in me" (Gal. 2:20). Through the self-absorbed teaching now passing for gospel truth in our churches, the true gospel of grace is blasphemously perverted. The result is that most Christians in contemporary culture have no concept of the biblical call to embrace suffering, sacrifice, and self-denial—which is not only a part of the Christian life-walk but, according to God's Word, is a gift and calling from our Lord to us. "For it has been granted to you that for the sake of Christ you should not only believe in him but also suffer for his sake" (Phil. 1:29). When such basic elements of the gospel life and Christ's calling are perverted at worst and remain untaught at best, how can the church possibly respond effectively to the challenges of today's world, and how can it possibly develop leaders who lead as servants and who willingly sacrifice themselves for others? Finally, as misguided church leaders follow a worldly, self-directed model of leadership, the spiritual depth of believers and the stability of their local churches are steadily eroded. In the pulpit, "tips for living" talks now replace gospel-driven and Christ-centered sermons. Personality traits trump character, and happiness trumps holiness. Perception trumps reality, and even the most sacred calling of the believer, divine worship, is replaced by personal entertainment. The congregation becomes the audience of spectators at the worship event. They arrive for the worship experience provided by the preacher and worship leaders, who are the primary actors, with God fulfilling the role of the set-up man. Not long ago, the church would have called this blasphemy. Today, we call it seeker-centered worship.

In contrast, true worship has an audience of One—the triune God. But not only does he receive our worship, he enters into it by providing the presence and power of the Holy Spirit who enables us to worship with passion for the praise of God. Too often today the biblical mandate to "worship the Father in spirit and truth" (John 4:23) is being replaced with a self-directed question: "How did that worship experience make me feel?" The result is that the divine service of worship has now become the human service of entertainment, and the focus is on the worshiper rather than the One who is to be worshiped. In reaction to this worldly trend, other congregations have descended into thoughtless traditionalism—steadfastly devoting themselves to comfortable, traditional worship practices with an exclusive fierceness that unwittingly promotes form over substance. Knowing how to worship God in spirit and truth while embracing seekers, teaching new believers,

17

and encouraging mature Christians requires godly leadership and is necessary to produce more godly leaders. Godly leaders are grown from the Word of God empowered by the Spirit of God as an inevitable result of God's grace—but they will not be raised up from today's corporate model of leadership, which has been baptized into the church.

To regain a biblical vision of leadership we must first regain lost ground by repenting of the thoughtless infusion of popular culture into the church life and leadership and also repenting of the absence of a biblical response to it. We must step back and turn away from popular trends and man-centered preoccupations while seriously surrendering to God's model of leadership found in Scripture. We have allowed the valid need of cultural contextualization to descend into cultural capitulation. The Word of God is not silent on leadership or how to develop and deploy leaders. God's Word is clear, and we must embrace the biblical vision, reclaiming the church as a leadership factory and distribution center by prioritizing the disciple-making task of *defining, developing,* and *deploying* Christian leaders in the American church.

An Immodest Proposal: 3-*D* Leadership

How do we begin? When we've repented and turned away from all the worldly models of leadership and the thoughtless imposition of man-centered leaders and leadership, what do we do next? How do we identify and implement biblical leadership in our denominations and local congregations? The answer: instead of following the whims of the world and the "spirit of the world" (1 Cor. 2:12), we must intentionally pursue a strategic commitment to three initiatives drawn from the timeless truth of God's Word and verified throughout history. I call these initiatives the "Three *Ds*" of biblical leadership: first, we must clearly *define* biblical leadership; second, we must *develop* godly leaders; and third, we must strategically *deploy* those leaders in the church and around the world.

18

Define

Having "put off" unbiblical worldly leadership we are now positioned to "put on" biblical leadership within the church. So let's define biblical leadership. An easy task, right? Actually, this is no small challenge because the truth of God's Word on leadership has been ignored, muted, or discarded in recent decades. A century ago—maybe even a generation ago—such biblical concepts as "many who are first will be last, and the last first" (Mark 10:31) were instantly understood and acknowledged by the people in the pews. No more. A lack of sound, systematic, biblical disciple making has produced contemporary congregations that are shockingly illiterate biblically. Thankfully, many want to be taught; many have a zeal and hunger for the truth. Furthermore, there is a hunger and longing for authentic leadership not only in the church today but also in the world. So the challenge is also an opportunity; existing leaders who have a passion for faithful and effective genuine biblical leadership can transform their congregations into leadership factories and distribution centers.

Doing so will no doubt demand a thoughtful and patient commitment. Biblical leaders must be sacrificial leaders, servant leaders, courageous leaders, beneficial leaders, nurturing leaders, combat leaders, compassionate leaders, and visionary leaders. They must be all of this—and through the sovereign grace of God, they can be. And when they put that kind of biblical leadership into practice, hearts and minds in the church will change. It's the "body of Christ"—that's how Scripture primarily pictures the church (e.g., 1 Cor. 12:27)—and the church will respond to the call of leadership reformation. The response will be a renewal of authentic unity—a unity of calling, a unity of salvation, a unity of the inspired Word of God, a unity in one Lord, one faith, one baptism. And this renewal of unity will also encourage a harmonious diversity of callings, passions, gifts, and abilities within the body of Christ.

There are two Greek words for *time* used in the Bible: *kairos* and *chronos*. *Chronos* denotes the chronological passing of time

19

while *kairos* denotes a season or opportune moment of time. The *kairos* leadership moment is now, and the church must not falter. As we define biblical leadership in the church, we should move simultaneously and strategically to define it for the world. We need to fully reverse what we have been doing. Instead of receiving the world's leaders defined and developed by worldly leadership models, the moment has arrived to define godly leadership for a cynical world and develop godly leaders who can be thoughtfully deployed into the world according to their God-given passions and desires. This is the moment to regain lost ground. There is a vacuum of good leadership, and a despair and cynicism about leadership. Notice, I did not say there is a vacuum of leadership but a vacuum of *good* leadership. God has called us to produce and propagate leaders who will be salt and light and bless society with courageous, trustworthy, and beneficial leadership. It has happened in history and has been demonstrated by the American church in centuries past. We must not drop the baton of biblical leadership disciple making that overflows into society, penetrating it with grace and truth.

Develop

When the biblical model of leadership is defined in our churches and denominational headquarters, then a new generation of leaders can be developed by disciple making. As the American church again comprehends what God expects of leadership, a new wave of leaders will arise—leaders who have been transformed by a biblical understanding of their task. And because biblical leaders by definition are multipliers, they will develop more leaders—leaders who have been mentored in God's church for distribution into the world: transformed leadership transforming others just as they themselves have been transformed, with each one multiplying and reproducing again and again and again. That's how God's leadership model works. We must reclaim this model again, and we must do it now.

Deploy

After the church has defined the biblical model of leadership and has begun developing leaders based on that model through leadership disciple making, then the church must be ready to deploy these emerging leaders into the world. Every institution of our contemporary culture should be influenced by these transformed leaders, who will be armed with the gospel of Jesus Christ, the truth of God's Word, and the love of Christ. If the biblical model of leadership disciple making is followed, Christian leaders will of necessity be deployed into every honorable sphere of society. These Christian leaders will be deployed according to their God-given gifts, talents, and passions. If some of these new leaders are in business, they will become Christian business leaders. If some are parents, they will produce Christ-centered families. If a leader is a husband, he will be the spiritual leader of his wife in Christ. Leaders in law enforcement and the military will understand how to protect those in their care and carry out their responsibilities with a biblical perspective. Christian attorneys will be prepared to advocate the cause of justice based on the historical Judeo-Christian worldview and will strive to restore a once-noble calling back to a position of respect. Elected officials and other officeholders will be equipped to exercise biblical leadership for the general welfare of society, and thankfully statesmen will replace politicians.

Contemporary culture would be transformed in an amazingly rapid span of time. The twentieth-century shift in American worldview from God-centered to man-centered could be reversed. What an exceptional gift of grace—from the risen Christ through his church. But we cannot have it both ways. Either we lead according to the world or we lead according to the Word. Those are our only choices. "Do not be conformed to this world, but be transformed . . ." (Rom. 12:2). The American church can step back from the edge of oblivion and avoid the deadly free fall that now faces us. Or not. By the grace of God, we still have time, and it is an opportune moment in time. An open door is before us. The failure of worldly leadership has demoralized our culture—so the church today is being offered a marvelous opportunity. By the grace of God, we can and we must seize the moment.

The book of Acts tells us that when Christian leaders such as Paul and Silas carried the truth of God's Word into the heart of the first-century Greco-Roman culture, they were met with this cry: "These men who have turned the world upside down have come here also" (Acts 17:6). How I would love to hear those words said one more time. Our problem, observed C. S. Lewis in *The Weight of Glory*, is that "Our Lord finds our desires not too strong, but too weak."[1] The Word of God drives home that point with even greater simplicity in Philippians 4:13: "I can do all things through [Christ] who strengthens me." Through the love of Jesus Christ, we are called by the God of the Bible to wrestle to the ground the death and decay that now cloak our culture. And his leadership manual stands ready and available. The cultural death spiral can be stopped, reversed, and transformed by gospel-driven and Christ-centered Christian leaders.

Define. Develop. Deploy. "Go therefore," God orders us, "and make disciples" (Matt. 28:19).

Now, what would these world-shaking leaders look like, where would they come from, and what would they do?

2

IN THE WORLD— BUT NOT *OF* THE WORLD

"You are the light of the world. . . .
Let your light shine before others,
so that they may see your good works
and give glory to your Father who is in heaven."
MATTHEW 5:14–16

t was a seemingly simple question.

"Where is your church?" a new acquaintance asked me.

"I don't know," I honestly replied.

"Well, how do you expect me to visit a church if the pastor doesn't even know where it is?" he asked good-naturedly.

"I do know the location where our church meets," I explained. "Now, as to where the church is right now, I don't know. Some of it may be at school. Some may be at a shopping mall. Or at home. Or maybe traveling—in cars, in airplanes. Some are all over the country, and a few are even in other parts of the world."

23

My point—which my new friend quickly grasped—was that the church is the people of God and that they are all over the place, engaged in lifestyle evangelism and disciple making. Our congregation meets in a certain location at various times, but *the members*—not a structure of brick and mortar—are the church. And the church, like each Christian, is commanded to be "in the world" but not "of the world" (John 17:11, 16).

Neither part of that commandment is easy. It's a genuine challenge to effectively follow Christ in the world around us, especially in a contemporary American culture where Christians are considered an irrelevant minority in an increasingly hostile environment. And in this technologically enhanced information society it's also increasingly difficult to keep from being conformed to the world around us—as individual believers and as congregations. One aspect of our God-created makeup is our inherent desire to fellowship with one another, and part of our sinful human nature is to constantly seek affirmation from each other. The ever-present temptation is to think that being "in Christ" is not sufficient and that we *must* have affirmation and approval from other human beings. This compulsion is so great it can often drive us to being man-pleasers rather than God-exalters.

Pitfalls from the World

Much of today's leadership in the church may be well intentioned, but is doomed to failure. Why? Because it is a leadership that has descended into cultural accommodation propelled by the desire for the culture's affirmation. In today's culture "god" is in but Jesus is out; spirituality is in but Christianity is out; religion is in but the gospel is out. In fact, Jesus, Christianity, and the gospel are more than "out," they are scandalous. The result of leaders desiring the affirmation of this contemporary culture is redefining Jesus from Lord and Savior of sinners to a therapist or a consultant for success in life—redefining Christianity in terms of success and self-promotion, and redefining the gospel in terms of material prosperity, pop psychology therapy, and a guide for self-help in life. Furthermore, these leaders are afraid to swim against the swelling tide of cultural opposition and even worse, they compromise the essence of the gospel and the call of the church for cultural affirmation. Today's leadership has lost confidence in the power of the Word of God, specifically the gospel. In fear of rejection and with an incessant need for popular affirmation, these leaders have injected the church with cultural steroids to make it "relevant and acceptable," hoping that somehow the result will be that people will then "accept" Jesus and the church will become bigger and stronger and therefore more influential. The sports world provides a ready example as some athletes desiring to be stronger or faster resort to the quick fix of steroids. They get the desired results rapidly, but at a great risk to their future and their health. Likewise, the tactics of cultural accommodation in the church by injecting the culture's driving values may temporarily inflate the numbers in the pews, but they move congregations toward destruction. "There is a way that seems right to a man," according to Proverbs 16:25, "but its end is the way to death." The church, "the body of Christ," injected with these cultural steroids may, like the athlete, gain immediate embellishments of size and acclaim but in reality these leaders have actually injected eventual disease and death into the body of believers they lead.

Of course we want to effectively communicate within the surrounding cultural context—whether our congregation is in Kenya or Kansas—but we must be determined not to substitute cultural acceptance for biblical faithfulness in the name of cultural contextualization and missional effectiveness. For instance, when worship shifts from being God-centered to being man-centered, it is because cultural accommodation has taken place, and the church leadership is choosing acceptance and supposed effectiveness over faithfulness and principle. When a church turns away from God-centered worship, even with seemingly noble motivations, it will eventually turn away from the very gospel itself. How can I be so sure of that? It's simple: the gospel is designed to disciple believers and bring them to a point of maturity in which they love "the praise of his glorious grace" (Eph. 1:6). When the body of Christ loses God-centered worship, it also loses the purpose of the gospel call, which is to bring praise and glory to God. Man-centered tactics may draw large numbers, but in fact, it's an illusion of growth. Using the same concept that draws large numbers to an athletic event or a rock concert does not insure effectiveness if the means are counterproductive to the content and purpose of the message and the mission. This kind of growth is described in 1 Corinthians 3:12 as "wood, hay, stubble" (KJV) instead of the "gold, silver, precious stones" created by Christ-centered disciple making.

Eventually comes destruction as the church loses its message and its mission. Methods always affect message. The Bible gives us many examples of cultural accommodation and its assured ultimate failure. Consider Lot, who was apparently a well-intentioned believer (2 Pet. 2:8). First, Lot "moved his tent as far as Sodom" (Gen. 13:12). Then we find him living in a "house" that is within the city. Eventually he is found sitting by the "gates of Sodom," which apparently meant that he had become a city elder. The insidious siren call of Sodom's culture gradually conformed Lot to that culture and suffocated his witness. When he finally spoke up on behalf of his guests, the disrespect of the city population surfaced with a vengeance and revealed a vehement hatred of the compromised man who, while being "vexed" in his righteous soul, had lost any witness and was in fact an object of ridicule. Not only did his accommodation fail to influence the surrounding culture, but he also lost the respect of his fellow citizens. That's obvious from the way the Sodomites mocked and threatened him when he sought to protect the visiting angels whom God had sent to rescue him and his family (Gen. 19:4–11). Instead of acting as the biblical light of the world, he was thoroughly assimilated into the secular culture—with no positive results. Not only did he fail to transform the culture, but the culture actually conformed *him* and his family.

Cultural Accommodation

This phenomenon is happening with astounding speed to the American church today. In the name of cultural relevance, many congregations have been guided by their leaders across the line into cultural accommodation. They have pitched their tent near Sodom. In fact, some church leaders have bought a house *in* Sodom, thinking that they're making the church and its message relevant when the opposite is true. Like Lot, church leaders who choose worldly models of leadership will eventually suffer a loss of respect and loss of voice, and so will their churches. Along the way—even while perhaps gaining numbers—these wayward church leaders will have also compromised their ability to equip their members to avoid falling into personal accommodation with the world. How tragic this inevitable consequence is for the members of the church and their families! Christians in America desperately need the local church to stay on task: to witness to the world without becoming like the world. Therefore there is a pressing need for leaders who will set the pace.

Cultural accommodation is easy today. Long gone is the day when the Judeo-Christian worldview defined our culture, encouraging individuals to do what was right and discouraging what was wrong. Living daily for the Lord is harder than ever in American culture. Passionate and faithful Christians are swimming against the cultural current on a host of national issues—and personal ones, too. The battle is not just with so-called social issues—the threat of same-sex marriage, the sanctity of life, or the loss of religious liberties, for instance—but also with issues that are down-home and up close and personal. For example, some parents in my church came to me with a real-life dilemma that might not have made the evening news, but was extremely important to them. It was also typical of what American believers and their families are battling today.

"Pastor Reeder," they explained, "we want to honor the Lord's Day, but our children's sports programs are on Sunday." We sat down and I listened to their story. Their local recreation league scheduled ball practice on Sundays. Should their families skip worship for ball practice? Should they pull their kids off the teams? Eventually they decided, appropriately, that obedience to Scripture and family worship on the Lord's Day was far more important than team sports. That may seem like an obvious choice to some readers, but it is not the norm. In the child-driven families of today's culture, it took courage and conviction to make the right decision—the kind of courage and conviction that church leaders must model if they desire to disciple and shepherd their members and their families.

As I led these parents through the Scriptures toward resolution of their problem, I thought about my own childhood in the American South in the 1950s. We had some significant cultural issues that needed to be addressed in that day and place, but having to choose between Sunday worship and ball practice wasn't one of them. In fact, sports programs not only avoided activities on Sundays, but would not even schedule practice or play on Wednesday nights when midweek church services were routinely held. Why not? Was the culture of the 1950s more sensitive to the worship and prayer schedule of the Christian church? Certainly it was, to a degree, but that wasn't the main reason that ball teams avoided Sunday and Wednesday night practice and play.

The main reason was that they wouldn't have had enough players to do anything if the committed Christians were absent. *And most would have been absent.* Christians connected in the society by playing in the community leagues of the day, but they also prioritized biblical obedience and commitment to Christ's church and Lord's Day worship. In response, the surrounding culture was affected by their faith and was shaped by it. Church leaders of the day taught that the Lord's Day was sacred—a gift from God—and was an essential means of grace in the life of a Christian. Under the influence of biblically based leadership, Christians used the Lord's Day to worship, rest, and be with their families. And unlike today, the parents' need for the child's friendship did not trump their call to be parents and make the right decision, even if it did not meet their child's approval. They didn't toss all of that aside to play ball. And if the Christians didn't show up, the ball teams couldn't function. Therefore, the athletic leagues adjusted their schedules to accommodate believers—not the reverse.

Not so today. Cultural accommodation by the church actually lessens our opportunity to impact the surrounding culture. Yes, some church leaders would argue that such accommodation enhances evangelism. But please remember that true effectiveness is never achieved at the expense of faithfulness! When a child's desire to play ball becomes more important to Christian parents than Sunday worship, the local church and its leadership are failing. The family is being "discipled" by the culture, instead of being discipled by the church. Assuredly we are commanded to connect with the surrounding culture, but we must do so through obedience to God's Word, not disobedience. Remember, we are called by our Lord to be "*in* the world" but "not *of* the world." Eventually, thoughtless *accommodation* to the world becomes *capitulation* to the world—and our witness for the Lord is rendered useless.

Traditionalism

On the other hand, church leaders must not let their congregations react to the trend of accommodation by plunging down the slippery slope of traditionalism. The reactionary trend of making the local church a religious museum of past achievements is equally unbiblical and ineffective. The church is to be a movement of the kingdom of God transforming the present and changing the future, not a monument of the past or a museum of religious nostalgia.

Think about it this way: A man decides to put his boat into a boat shed because he does not want it to sink. He's right—the boat won't sink if it's in the boat shed. But it's also absolutely useless as a boat. If the church is taken out of the world in an attempt to avoid compromise, it may not be guilty of accommodation, but—like the boat—it will be useless. Such unbiblical reactionary leadership in the contemporary American church either isolates members from the world in order to stay "pure" and on message or encourages them to accommodate the world in the mistaken notion of being "relevant and effective." Instead of this deficient leadership, American Christians need transformational leaders who trust the Holy Spirit and the power of the Word and are living examples of it.

God's Way

We need to avoid sliding down the treacherous slope of accommodation on one side and the equally dangerous slope of traditionalism and isolation on the other. Instead, God's call is for us to be at the pinnacle—the point of tension—that is God's truth lived and proclaimed in love. We can't achieve this alone; it requires knowing the Word and trusting in the power of the Spirit of God. That's where biblical leadership does the Lord's work: proclaiming the gospel and making disciples according to the Word and through the Holy Spirit. Remember, God's transforming grace meets people right where they are. Nobody has to get "better" to come to Jesus. This glorious truth of Scripture is summarized well in the words of the great hymn: "Just as I am, without one plea," and affirmed in the hymn, "Rock of Ages," which declares, "Nothing in my hands I bring, simply to thy cross I cling." And praise the Lord, when we come to him just as we are, he will never leave us as we are. We're saved by faith alone, through grace alone, in Christ alone—but because of the love of Christ, faith and grace never remain alone. When those whom God has saved are enabled through biblical leadership to grow by grace, then the transforming power of the gospel at work within them and upon them will flow from their lips and their lives, attracting and drawing men and women from the world to Christ and his kingdom as they "seek to save the lost" (Luke 19:10).

God's grace is glorious, all-powerful, and as the hymn writer declares, "greater than all our sins." It not only redeems sinners but transforms them. Grace-filled leaders will become transformed leaders, and eventually they become transformational leaders.

Then, committed to true evangelism and disciple making, they will unleash God's church as a change agent in the surrounding society. It happened with Moses, David, and Paul—and it can still happen today when we *define*, *develop*, and *deploy* such leaders in the church and send them into the world. This transforming power of the gospel changes men and women. When they change, their families change. When families change, their neighborhoods change. When neighborhoods change, cities change. When cities change, nations change. And when nations change, the world is turned upside down.

Let us begin here and now. We live in a new dark age. Yet we must remember that light shines most brightly in darkness. We have a great opportunity before us to return light to our darkened nation. To do so, we *must* put aside what is false and embrace what is true. Let us put aside the false promises of cultural accommodation and the false security of traditionalism. We must start by embracing the truth through intentionally implementing the biblical model of faithful and effective Christ-centered and gospel-driven multiplication leaders who produce followers of Christ who also are gospel-driven and Christ-centered followers of Christ "in the world" but not "of the world." In our present darkness, let there be light—the light of the gospel of Christ shining forth from his church like a "city set on a hill" (Matt. 5:14). How do we get there? It is astoundingly simple. Christ, in his three-year ministry, gave us the ministry paradigm as he intentionally prioritized defining, developing, and deploying leaders who would produce leaders who would amazingly impact a hostile and pagan world through gospel evangelism and disciple making—leaders who would not seek cultural affirmation but instead achieve cultural transformation. In a word—Christian leaders who are worldshakers. So where do they come from?

3

HIS WAYS ARE NOT OUR WAYS—THANKFULLY!

"For my thoughts are not your thoughts,
neither are your ways my ways, declares the LORD."

ISAIAH 55:8

Who was the target audience for the Sermon on the Mount?

The five thousand? You? Me? All of us? Each of those answers is correct, of course, because the Holy Spirit has been changing hearts with those words ever since the Lord spoke them. When Jesus delivered his Sermon on the Mount, however, he was speaking first to his disciples. Matthew introduces the Sermon on the Mount with these words: "Seeing the crowds, [Jesus] went up on the mountain, and when he sat down, *his disciples* came to him. And he opened his mouth and taught them, saying . . ." (Matt. 5:1–2). The Sermon on the Mount was a discipleship sermon, and it was directed first to the twelve leaders whom Jesus had chosen. Obviously, he was aware of the multitudes on the hillside listening to him but target audience number one was the Twelve.

In fact, if you carefully study the life of Christ in the Scriptures, you'll see that the major investment of the Lord's disciple making on earth was spent on leadership development. He actually focused on training three specific groups of leaders. He discipled them, developed them, and—at his ascension—deployed them. Who were the three groups? You can see them clearly in the Gospels: the Seventy, the Twelve, and the Three. He defined leadership by "doing and teaching." He then developed these people as leaders through discipling them, and then he deployed them into the world, and within a quarter of a century the civilized world would be turned upside down.

The Incarnation Leadership Model

When the Lord Jesus Christ came into this world, he took upon himself a physical body, and God became a true man. In that body he was fully God and fully man, and in that body he went to the cross to redeem his people, to defeat Satan and the principalities of darkness, and to purchase a triumphant church. In fulfilling this mission he simultaneously displayed a model of leadership and implemented a strategy for leadership multiplication. This is the model of leadership that the American church needs today—a model that if implemented will impact the world. Almost two thousand years ago Jesus initiated the model of Three-*D* leadership—he *defined*, *developed*, and *deployed* leaders who in turn implemented the same model so that within less than a generation the known world is turned upside down.

Think about what he did as heaven's Champion, our Redeemer, in fulfilling his threefold incarnation mission. First, he came into the world to save sinners. "She will bear a son, and you shall call his name Jesus," reports Matthew 1:21, "for he will save his people from their sins." First Timothy 1:15 also states this aspect of his mission with pointed clarity: "The saying is trustworthy and deserving of full acceptance, that Christ Jesus came into the world to save sinners. . . ." Second, he came to destroy the works of Satan—the principalities and powers of darkness. "The reason the Son of God appeared was to destroy the works of the devil," according to 1 John 3:8. Jesus' third missional objective was to purchase his church militant, triumphant, and ultimately victorious—as referenced in Ephesians 5:25–27: "Husbands, love your wives, as Christ loved the church and gave himself up for her, . . . so that he might present the church to himself in splendor, without spot or wrinkle or any such thing, that she might be holy and without blemish." We also see this in Acts 20:28: "Pay careful attention to yourselves and to all the flock, in which the Holy Spirit has made you overseers, to care for the church of God, which he obtained with his own blood."

Saving us sinners. Destroying the works of Satan. Establishing his victorious church on earth. And embedded in achieving his threefold mission is the strategy of leadership multiplication of servant leaders for the kingdom.

Satan, observing Christ's plan and priority upon intentional leadership multiplication, not only attacks the worship of God and the church on its mission but he also attacks the leaders of the church. That's why the apostle Paul warned the elders at Ephesus (Acts 20:17–34) that Satan would seek to penetrate the leadership of the church: "I know that after my departure fierce wolves will come in among you, not sparing the flock; and from among your own selves will arise men speaking twisted things, to draw away the disciples after them" (v. 29). Paul called them to be faithful shepherds and not allow Satan to infiltrate them with false teachers and self-centered leaders. The victory of Christ in fulfilling his mission was declared at the resurrection, the Great Commission was initiated at his ascension, and the model for leadership and leadership multiplication was displayed throughout his ministry—and the result was that the world "turned upside down" (Acts 17:6) in less than twenty-five years. You can almost feel the frustration of the man who uttered these words in his analysis of what had happened through the power of the gospel, the Holy Spirit, and a church on mission that included servant leader multiplication of transformational leaders as modeled by Christ himself. It has had a God-made impact unlike anything else that ever happened in the history of humanity, and it was only the beginning.

Uncounted millions of people have been transformed from spiritual death to life by the gospel of Jesus Christ. Nations have been established, reformed, and some destroyed and, by its impact. Political and economic systems have arisen, undergone refinement, diminished, or disappeared because of its influence. Ministry movements have transformed lives and cultures throughout the world and through the ages. The gospel, moved forward by Christ's model of leadership, has reverberated through history, so much so that the Western world has divided time into BC and AD—"before Christ" and *anno Domini* ("in the year of the Lord"). Meanwhile, the body of Christ—the church—has by the grace of God withstood widespread rejection, persecution, mass martyrdom, internal failures, and unfaithful followers.

If a human world leader or a multinational corporation tried to affect the world in a comparatively minor way today, consultants would be summoned to develop an international marketing strategy. A worldwide database would have to be constructed. Mass media would have to be deployed—advertising campaigns, Web sites, multimedia tactics, marketing tools, news media liaisons, branding, direct mail—all of man's methods of modern communications. But that's not what Jesus did. In fact, Jesus repeatedly walked away from the multitudes and told people to be silent about what he had done. He never personally wrote a single thing, except for once when he wrote in the sand. God's way and the world's way are not the same. The Word of God says: "For my thoughts are not your thoughts, neither are your ways my ways, declares the LORD" (Isa. 55:8).

Jesus had the Seventy, he called the Twelve, and he focused on the Three (Peter, James, and John). Then they continued the model implemented by Christ. Peter, along with Barnabas, helped to define, develop, and deploy a future leader named Saul of Tarsus, who was renamed Paul. Eventually, in turn, Paul's leadership team was large, profound, and effective. Not content with that, when his time to leave this world approached, he prepared another new leader to carry his ministry forward. His name was Timothy—and with these inspired words, Paul charged him to continue defining, developing, deploying: "You then, my child, be strengthened by the grace that is in Christ Jesus, and what you have heard from me in the presence of many witnesses entrust to faithful men who will be able to teach others also" (2 Tim. 2:1–2). And all of this recorded in the New Testament had Old Testament precedent.

God's providence prior to the sending of Christ into the world had promoted this paradigm of defining, developing, and deploying leaders throughout the Old Testament. Moses defined, developed, and deployed leaders such as the elders and Joshua and Caleb. David had his three mighty men and his thirty men of renown. Elijah had his Elisha and his school of the prophets. The model Christ revealed in his incarnation had been embedded in the Old Testament and fully implemented in the New Testament. Its effectiveness as a strategy was affirmed even by its frustrated adversaries, and it needs to be reestablished in the church today—and the opportunity is before us.

I would love to hear an adversary again say even in frustration "these people who have turned the world upside down have come here also." If we desire to hear this, we must not only exalt Christ in word and deed, we must prioritize defining, developing, and deploying leaders. "These people" who were world-shapers did not just appear; they were intentionally developed, and they have kept appearing throughout history.

The Model at Work

Not only does the Bible record this incarnational model of leadership, but we see it providentially working throughout church history. God raised up Martin Luther to initiate the Reformation. Luther developed leaders such as Ulrich Zwingli, Philipp Melanchthon, and hundreds of others who made the Reformation a roaring stream of gospel truth reforming the church and spreading throughout the world. John Calvin's devotion to producing leaders for world evangelism was extraordinary: he developed thirteen hundred missionaries just for France alone and even sent a team of trained leaders to take the gospel to what is today Rio de Janeiro, Brazil. John Knox multiplied his leadership with his "black-robed militia"—gospel preachers in Geneva gowns whom he had trained to live out his prayer that God would "give me Scotland" (for Christ).

As leaders multiplied from the Reformation just in time for the age of discovery, the revival jumped the Atlantic and spilled into North America. It laid the groundwork culture for the thirteen colonies and led to the Great Awakening in eighteenth-century America. Providentially, that remarkable revival prepared Americans for independence and laid a spiritual foundation for American culture and government. It also returned a blessing to England, sparing it from the humanism that smothered France in the French Revolution and spurring more English evangelism. In turn, as leaders multiplied leaders, the Christian church in America spawned a massive missionary movement that eventually covered most of the globe and is even now transforming Africa, South America, and, amazingly, Asia.

God's ways are not our ways—indeed. That's why the leaders of the contemporary American church must return to the Christ-given model of leadership and leadership multiplication of transformational leaders who will multiply others also. Leaders identifying leaders, molding leaders, and multiplying leaders. It's God's strategy modeled by Christ, embedded in the Old Testament, implemented by the apostles, reclaimed by the Reformation, and gloriously practiced in the Great Awakening. But what has happened today? It will produce fruit unlike anything we can copy from the world. As we begin anew, let us beseech the Lord our God with this prayer: "Lord, please launch a movement of grace for the kingdom of God in our midst and in our day. Father! Please! Do it again, and do it with us!"

And what do these multiplication leaders look like when they are defined, developed, and deployed through Christ-centered disciple making? Thankfully, again, the Scriptures are not silent. Christ, in his life and with his Word, has not only given us an effective strategy, he has also profiled what these leaders look like. So, first things first. Before we can develop and deploy such worldshaking leaders, we need to define them. The marks of such gospel-driven leaders are profoundly profiled in God's Word. Let's look closely at them.

4

DEFINING THE LEADER

"The people had a mind to work. . . . And the leaders
stood behind the whole house of Judah,
who were building the wall. . . ."

NEHEMIAH 4:6, 16–18

Preachers love Peter.

He's the best known of the twelve apostles not just because he achieved so much, but also because he messed up so much. His stumbling ways remind those of us in leadership just how easy it is to fall flat on our faces. The biblical accounts of his sins, mistakes, and human frailties provide a rich record of erroneous examples that cautions us to live carefully, and his ready repentance and transparent declarations encourage us all. Peter often seemed to have an open-mouth–insert-foot problem (only to Peter did the Lord say in Matthew 16:23, "Get behind me, Satan!"), but it was actually less the "foot in his mouth" than it was the "heart in his mouth." Peter was a well-intended believer who acted on impulse and passion and therefore was in desperate need of discipling not only as a follower of Christ but also as a future leader for Christ. The Lord corrected and redirected Peter more often than any other disciple in the biblical record. Yet many times, Peter's heart was in harmony with the will of his Savior. For example, when disciples were falling away, the Lord asked the Twelve if they wanted to go, too. "Lord, to whom shall we go?" Peter said. "You have the words of eternal life, and we have believed, and have come to know, that you are the Holy One of God" (John 6:68–69). Why did Peter and the others stay? Why did they not leave him to follow someone else? One element of the answer is the Lord's leadership, which inspired them to stay the course and give their lives without reservation to him and to his mission.

The mission is the Great Commission, to "make disciples of all nations" (Matt. 28:19), and church history indicates that almost all of them gave away their lives by following it. These opinionated men—who were politically, economically, regionally, and religiously diverse—came to Christ, were given new life by him, and then followed his leading with remarkable focus. One (Judas) was lost to apostasy, but the other eleven (along with Matthias, Paul, and the newly converted brothers of Jesus) gave themselves to the mission, and along with those, they developed and deployed leaders who "turned the world upside down" (Acts 17:6). Lesson learned? We learn and implement leadership by first embracing Christ as the model of a leader, one who develops and empowers other leaders.

Toward Defining a Leader

Now the eleven disciples went to Galilee, to the mountain to which Jesus had directed them. And when they saw him they worshiped him, but some doubted. And Jesus came and said to them, "All authority in heaven and on earth has been given to me. Go therefore and make disciples of all nations, baptizing them in the name of the Father and of the Son and of the Holy Spirit, teaching them to observe all that I have commanded you.

And behold, I am with you always, to the end of the age." (Matt. 28:16–20)

In his earthly ministry, Jesus showed us what a leader is, how a leader intentionally produces other leaders, and how they remain focused and unified on their mission. Matthew 28:16–20 contains the concept of a leader as Christ's chosen and developed leaders are given their mission to not only achieve for Christ but also give away to others until the "end of the age" and Christ's return.

A leader influences others to effectively achieve a defined mission together.

Let's think about that statement. Three key words stand out in the definition and in the observation of Jesus' leadership: *influence*, *effective*, and *together*. Let's examine them one at a time.

Influence

The first key word is *influence*. Diagram 4.1 is a simple illustration of what's needed to be a leader who effectively influences others who in turn become influential leaders also.

Diagram 4.1 An Influencer Is A:

Model	➡	**By Embodiment**	➡	**For Imitation**
Mentor	➡	**By Education**	➡	**For Instruction**
Motivator	➡	**By Empowerment**	➡	**For Inspiration**
Manager	➡	**By Equipping**	➡	**For Implementation**
Minister	➡	**By Evaluation**	➡	**For Improvement**

You can see that an influencer must accomplish five tasks in a specific order. Each task also requires five leadership skills.

First, leaders influence others by *embodiment* to take advantage of our commitment to *imitation*. Thus, a leader must develop the skill of being a *model*. For instance, if a leader doesn't model integrity, then he or she may be dismissed as a hypocrite, no matter what he or she teaches about integrity. There's truth to the adage "let your walk match your talk." Christian leaders must live what they teach—modeling is the key to the opportunity to mentor and teach leaders. In Acts 1, Luke refers to the life of Jesus, which Luke recorded in his Gospel as being a record of what Jesus "began to do and teach" (Acts 1:1). In disciple making, Jesus would model and then mentor. For instance, when the disciples saw Jesus pray, they asked him to "teach us to pray." Effective disciple making in general and leadership discipling in particular requires consistent modeling to open the door and solidify effective mentoring. "Doing" in the life of a leader is the gateway to "teaching" in the lives of future leaders.

Consider this illustration: Although babies have the capacity to communicate, they don't have a particular language gene programmed into their DNA. Yet within a few years, they learn to speak a native tongue. They're taught a language by a nonprofessional (usually a mother), who typically has not been trained to achieve this amazing feat. So how is that possible? First, the baby is nurtured and encouraged by a mother's persevering love. Second, all humans are born imitators. Paul writes in 1 Corinthians 4:15–16: "For I became your father in Christ Jesus through the gospel. I urge you, then, be imitators of me." According to some estimates, 80 percent of what is learned comes through imitation and 20 percent by instruction. The 20 percent is crucial because it establishes what ought to be imitated and how to conserve it, but most of what we learn is acquired by imitation. Therefore, being a model with character integrity is a priority.

Second, a leader influences others by *education*. People cannot do the right thing no matter how much they admire it in the life of another until they know the right thing; therefore, good leaders influence by *education* for the purpose of *instruction*. To do this, a leader must develop the skills of a *mentor*. For example, the book of Acts reports that the evangelist Apollos was inspired and passionate for the Lord's work, but had inaccurate knowledge. Two leaders who had been developed by Paul—Aquila and Priscilla—"took [Apollos aside] and explained to him [mentored] the way of God more accurately" (Acts 18:26). They influenced him. Great leaders become skillful mentors so that they can influence others by education for the purpose of instruction.

An influencer's third task is to *inspire* new leaders by *empowerment*. A leader who desires to empower and inspire must develop the skill of a *motivator*. In the deadly trench warfare of World War I, Colonel Douglas MacArthur—who, as General MacArthur, would drive Imperial Japanese forces across the Pacific in World War II—was ordered to cross "no-man's land" and assault a German-fortified position. All previous efforts to take the post had failed. MacArthur knew that success—and survival—depended on his leadership. He assigned his second-in-command, an army major, the task of leading the charge against the left flank of the enemy position. "Sir, I place you on the left side," MacArthur explained. "I will lead from the center." Then having been a model for leadership and having mentored this young leader to follow him as he led from the center, MacArthur moved from modeling and mentoring to being a motivator. "I know that you are capable of leading the men on to victory," he told the major. Then MacArthur pointed to a medal awarded for courage that was pinned on his uniform. "When this battle is over," he said, "I'll see to it that you get one of these." He turned and walked away—then spun around and strode back to the young officer. He quickly removed his medal and pinned it on the surprised major. "I know what kind of man you are," MacArthur told him. "I'm not going to wait for the end of this battle to give you this medal. Here, I'll give you mine now. I'll see you at the top." What do you think that man accomplished? He took the enemy position—in part because MacArthur had influenced him through embodiment, education, and empowerment.

The fourth strategy of an influencer is *equipping* for the purpose of *implementation*. In order to equip, the leader must become a good *manager*. As a manager, the leader provides resources needed for people to do what they've been called to do. Nothing is more frustrating than calling people to a mission without equipping them to do the work. An effective leader will manage the ultimate delivery of the resources and equipment necessary to complete the mission.

An influencer's final strategic challenge is *evaluation* for the purpose of *improvement*. Leaders must love those they lead enough to make time for both celebration and evaluation when a leadership task has been accomplished. This requires the heart and skill of a *minister* servant and ensures personal development and improvement. It's wrong-headed and wrong-hearted for leaders of other leaders to move on to the next task without promoting celebration of a completed effort and evaluation for improvement in the lives of those who have served on the team of leaders. To press on without taking the time for celebration and evaluation is demoralizing and therefore counterproductive. Christian leadership celebrates God's glory as well as the success of others. Christian leaders evaluate so that those who have served effectively can find ways for improvement and growth. Evaluation reveals strengths and weaknesses and establishes plans for personal development and growth. This critical step must not be omitted for the sake of moving on to the next objective, and it must be implemented both for morale and the opportunity for meaningful growth in the lives of those who are being developed as leaders.

Effectiveness

The second key word for developing leaders is *effectiveness*. Corporate America highlights efficiency. Christian leadership promotes first faithfulness, then effectiveness, and then and only then, efficiency. Efficiency is useless if you are not effective and to be effective requires faithfulness. The following four steps can achieve the development of future leaders who are what I like to call *FEE*: Faithful, Effective, and therefore meaningfully Efficient.

1. The principle of effectiveness: learning to do the right things.

2. The principle of excellence: learning to do the right things in the right way.
3. The principle of efficiency: learning to do the right things in the right way at the right time.
4. The principle of exaltation: learning to do the right things in the right way at the right time for the right reasons.

The first principle is that of *effectiveness*: a commitment to doing the *right things*. In today's society, leaders are encouraged to learn efficiency for the purpose of multitasking—but doing the right thing is more important than doing many things. Consider this modified example from the book *First Things First:*[1] A professor set a large glass cylinder in front of his class. In it were several large rocks, with two even larger rocks that would not fit inside sitting nearby on the professor's desk.

"Is the jar full," he asked the class, "or can I fit the additional rocks into the container?" Most students agreed that the jar was full. The professor then shook it, causing the rocks to settle and making room for one more rock.

"Is the jar full now?" he asked.

"Yes, no more rocks will fit into the jar," the students concluded.

The professor then produced a container of sand from beneath the desk and poured the sand into the cylinder. The sand settled into the spaces between the rocks.

"Is the jar full now?" he asked.

"No," said most of the class members, who had figured out the professor's technique. Sure enough, he next poured water into the jar. It soaked into the sand and finally filled the cylinder.

"So what lessons did you learn?" the professor asked. One student suggested that there's always room to squeeze in a little more.

"True," agreed the professor, "that's the lesson of efficiency—you can usually squeeze a little more activity into life—but that's not the main lesson." The students looked puzzled. "The main point," the professor concluded, "is that big rocks must go in first. That's the principle of effectiveness. To be truly effective, you must identify the big rocks in your life and place them as a priority in your finite life calendar."

So what are the "big rocks" in your life, the ones that must be given first place in your life calendar? For Christian leaders the big rocks are the biblically revealed responsibilities and relationships that are crucial to effective living for the glory of God. They cannot be squeezed into life as an afterthought. Space must be allocated for them as a priority. For example, a Christian realizes that daily time with the Lord in prayer and in the Word is one of the big rocks. So is worship on the Lord's Day. Time with one's spouse is a big rock. The parent-child relationship is, too. In other words, God's priorities—as taught in his Word—are the big rocks that we must give first place in our life calendars. This is what establishes the principle of effectiveness—making and intentionally keeping a commitment to do the right things. Take your calendar and put in the "big rocks" first.

The second principle of effective leadership is a commitment to *excellence—doing the right things in the right way*. When we stand before our Savior, what do we want to hear him say? "Well done, good and faithful servant," right? That's our desire, according to Matthew 25:21. Notice that the first word in that statement is *well*—the principle of excellence. That's more than just *done*, more than being acceptable or mediocre. "Well done" is what we want to hear the Lord say to us. Few of us will ever be the best at anything, but all of us can *do* our best. That's what we do when we do the right things in the right way as an offering of praise to our glorious Savior.

My parents—and yours, too, probably—used to say, "Son, if it's worth doing, it's worth doing right." That's the principle of excellence. The right thing (effectiveness) is worth doing, and it's worth doing in the right way (excellence).

Next is the principle of *efficiency—doing the right thing in the right way at the right time*—or doing more than one thing at a time when it's appropriate. Today it's called "multitasking," but when done correctly, it's still the principle of efficiency. When I was a child, my father, who was in baseball, arranged for me to be excused from school for two weeks to join him on a road trip. It was exciting to watch him at work and to be able to spend time with him. When I had children of my own, this was one way in which I wanted to imitate my father. So I usually tried to take one of my children with me when I led a conference or went on a short-term mission trip, or visited someone in the hospital. This allowed me to fulfill my calling as a pastor/teacher while also spending meaningful time with one of my children, and it was one of the blessings of the principle of efficiency thoughtfully applied. Another way in which I've tried to apply this principle is by extending it to disciple making by taking others with me on hospital calls, mission trips, and ministry opportunities. I usually invite members of our church leadership team to join me, so that not only am I fulfilling my pastoral ministry, I'm also including others—which blesses me and assists ministry efficiency while it hones their leadership skills as we debrief the experience and consider the Lord's blessings and life's lessons.

The concluding principle of *exaltation* is simply *learning to do everything for the right reasons.* The first and foremost reason is "to glorify God and enjoy him forever" (Westminster Catechism question and answer 1). The second reason is for the edification—the building up—of others. For instance, Ephesians 4:29 states that we are to communicate with other believers not in order to "vent" or "get something off my chest"—which is a self-directed motive—but instead to "give grace to those who hear." It's part of the biblical call to be an encourager, which is summarized in 1 Thessalonians 5:11: "Therefore encourage one another and build one another up, just as you are doing."

This twofold principle of exaltation is reflected in the Great Commandment: "love the Lord your God with all your heart and with all your soul and with all your mind . . . [and] love your neighbor as yourself" (Matt. 22:37–39). We see this principle modeled by the apostles John and Paul. According to Scripture, the apostle John "rejoiced greatly to find some of your children walking in the truth" (2 John 4), and the apostle Paul's zeal to glorify the Lord was inseparably connected to a concern for the well-being of others.

One final thought on effectiveness. As Christians, and especially as Christian leaders, we should reject the concept of "managing" time in favor of "spending" time. We never want to squander the precious resource of time, but spending it means focusing on investing it joyously, wisely, and unselfishly—rather than always trying to "beat the clock." We are born into this world with a finite number of sunrises and sunsets. While many resources are renewable, our days are not. They don't need to be managed—we need to be managed. The Scripture calls us to "redeem the time." Once we "spend" a day or even an hour or a moment, we do not get that back—so spend them effectively with a commitment to excellence that embraces efficiency and maintains the exaltation of God as well as the encouragement of others. We don't usually fail because we can't do more than one thing at a time; we fail because too often we don't do the right thing in the right way at the right time for the right reasons. Biblical leadership encourages others to do the right thing in the right way at the right time for the right reasons.

Togetherness

When a Christian servant leader influences others to effectively achieve a defined mission, then people will bond together as a team. These four principles of effective leadership will also bring people *together* when they embrace the mission as a team. Okay, you may logically ask, having motivational unity is an obvious necessity, but how else does a team achieve success? How does a team properly complete its mission? Again, the answer lies in the biblical model of leadership, summarized in three powerful and unifying team building dynamics.

First, a unified, motivated team has to accept the team leader. A title does not a leader make. It's only when people follow that a leader can truly lead. So one of the responsibilities of a leader is placing members on the right team. If some team members don't accept the leader, they should be encouraged to seek another team, no matter how valuable they may appear to be. Diversity brings strength, but only with unity—and team unity begins with acceptance of the team leader. The leader must be supported, embraced, encouraged, and followed by the team.

A second factor in bringing people together is unified acceptance of the team's defined mission. Without an accepted mutual objective, a team cannot function. It cannot score. This means that team members should put aside personal agendas and embrace the mission along with the leader.

Third, it's also crucial for team members to accept one another. To successfully complete the mission, team members should appreciate each other and each other's responsibilities. This means that all team members should look for opportunities to support each other, in good times and bad alike.

These three factors make individuals into a team rather than a mob or just a group. A team leader must consistently teach these factors and unrelentingly promote them. One of the most memorable illustrations of the impact of these three factors is found in the book of Nehemiah. The Lord gave Nehemiah, the leader, the vitally important mission of rebuilding the wrecked wall of Jerusalem. The people accepted his leadership. They accepted the mission. They accepted each other. And they achieved success. Their humble, determined attitude honored the Lord and made them an effective team. When they unified in accepting Nehemiah as their leader, collectively embracing the mission and accepting one another as team members, they were empowered—and they rebuilt the wall of Jerusalem as God intended. The Word of God notes the result: "the people had a mind to work" (Neh. 4:6).

The result is that they worked together as a team. Most teams consist of disconnected people doing their task and hoping it works out. I compare them to golf teams. On a golf team each golfer plays his own game, and then everyone adds up all of their scores at the end. Good teams are more like football teams. Everyone has a responsibility, but all are playing the same game and attempting to score by crossing the same goal line. Not only do you have your personal assignment but you also have a responsibility to assist one another. The *team* scores. The *team* wins. The *team* crosses the goal line—together. If a great catch was made in the end zone, the quarterback threw it, the offensive line protected the quarterback, other receivers distracted the defense, and the result is that the *team* scores—not just the person who caught the ball. So it can be for us today. Imagine what would happen to our culture—our world—if it could be said of the contemporary American church that in the name of Jesus Christ, "the people had a mind to work"—together.

Not only are leaders marked by the ability to influence others to effectively achieve a defined mission together, but of necessity they also have absolutely nonnegotiable personal qualities required for long-term effective leadership. Christian leadership is a privilege, not a right, and is attached to one's progress in the gospel; it does not come about simply because one has been converted by the gospel. What does that gospel-driven progress look like?

5

THE MARKS OF AN EFFECTIVE CHRISTIAN LEADER

"Therefore an overseer must be above reproach. . . ."
1 TIMOTHY 3:2

They're hard to miss.

They're the foundation texts on formal leadership in the church, some of the most familiar passages in Scripture. They're easy to find. They're easy to understand. And, alas, they're also too often ignored. With saddening frequency, Christian congregations and church authorities repeatedly choose leaders based on their occupations, personalities, or professional achievements, rather than the biblical qualifications for leadership. The result? Church congregations remain spiritually immature. False doctrine is taught. Biblical truth is neglected. Pastors are dismissed. Churches split apart. Members are distracted, disgruntled, or disheartened. The work of the church grows cold and the opportunity to model and mentor leaders in the church for deployment into the world is squandered.

Lack of leadership is tragic. Bad leadership and worldly leaders are disastrous. Meanwhile, God's leadership requirements remain unknown and unheeded. Biblical truth transforms, but it must be known and applied. So what are the key texts on the required marks of a Christian leader? There are two texts designed to provide a foundation point for profiling the essential marks of a leader. We must remember that if we don't commit, by God's grace, to develop Christian leaders as profiled in God's Word for the church, then we will not and, in fact, we cannot produce Christian leaders to deploy into the world.

> The saying is trustworthy: If anyone aspires to the office of overseer, he desires a noble task. Therefore an overseer must be above reproach, the husband of one wife, sober-minded, self-controlled, respectable, hospitable, able to teach, not a drunkard, not violent but gentle, not quarrelsome, not a lover of money. He must manage his own household well, with all dignity keeping his children submissive, for if someone does not know how to manage his own household, how will he care for God's church? He must not be a recent convert, or he may become puffed up with conceit and fall into the condemnation of the devil. Moreover, he must be well thought of by outsiders, so that he may not fall into disgrace, into a snare of the devil. (1 Tim. 3:1–7)

> This is why I left you in Crete, so that you might put what remained into order, and appoint elders in every town as I directed you—if anyone is above reproach, the husband of one wife, and his children are believers and not open to the charge of debauchery or insubordination. For an overseer, as God's steward, must be above reproach. He must not be arrogant or quick-tempered or a drunkard or violent or greedy for gain, but hospitable, a lover of good, self-controlled, upright, holy, and disciplined. He must hold firm to the trustworthy word as taught, so that he may be able to give instruction in sound doctrine and also to rebuke those who contradict it. (Titus 1:5–9)

Compiling these two key texts enables us to identify four required marks for Christian leaders in the church who will position the church to produce world-changing leaders who are able to impact every sphere of society. If these four marks of a Christian leader are neglected then the deployment of impact leaders for the world will be nothing more than an abandoned idea.

Four Leadership Requirements

The first requirement for leadership in God's church is the existence of a divine "call." This means that *the leader seeks the position, the position does not seek the leader*. According to Scripture, there are two aspects of a biblical call: internal and external. The internal call is given by the Holy Spirit to motivate the leader with a God-given passion and spiritual gifts. The internal call is described in 1 Timothy 3:1: "if anyone *aspires* to the office of overseer, he *desires* a noble task." Note the words *aspires* and *desires*. God moves in the hearts of potential leaders to equip them with a God-given passion to lead and a selfless sense of calling to be a leader. The word *selfless* is crucial. A call is not the drive of an inflated ego or the maneuvering of a manipulator to control others or gain power. The church is in need of leaders who desire the work of a leader not simply the position or title of a leader.

A leader's call is also *external*. If any leader senses that he has an internal call, he should submit himself to the leadership and fellowship of the church for verification and affirmation. As Romans 10:15 observes concerning preaching leaders, "how are they to preach unless they are sent?" Leaders must have the affirmation of those who have mentored and observed them. Those whom they would lead and those who would be their colleagues in leadership must be able to affirm the internal call with an external call. Therefore a leader should be both called and affirmed—internally called by the Holy Spirit, externally called by Spirit-led church leaders and members. It's a humbling experience to submit to the evaluation of the church and its formal leaders, but it's also liberating and empowering. Jesus Christ, who humbled himself to come into this world, commands us to submit and exercise humility—and that includes aspiring leaders. "Humble yourselves, therefore, under the mighty hand of God so that at the proper time he may exalt you" (1 Pet. 5:6).

A second leadership requirement is this: *Godliness is more important than giftedness.* While being gifted is important, a gifted leader who lacks godliness can lead others to destruction. Godliness is crucial. "An overseer must be above reproach" (1 Tim. 3:2). When God develops the heart of a leader, there's evidence of grace-saturated character, which produces godliness. A leader's character is forged from loving submission to the One who possesses him, his life, and his leadership.

The third requirement for leadership is equally important: *Effective leaders must develop a grace-driven and disciplined lifestyle.* According to 1 Timothy 3:2–7, a leader must display a discernible pattern of discipline. He should personally be above reproach in lifestyle conduct ("Therefore an overseer must be above reproach, the husband of one wife, sober-minded, self-controlled, respectable, hospitable, able to teach," v. 2) and his household should display a faithful and focused, God-centered environment ("He must manage his own household well, with all dignity keeping his children submissive, for if someone does not know how to manage his own household, how will he care for God's church?" vv. 4–5). Then according to verse 6, this leader should not be a "novice" or a "recent convert," which means that the lifestyle of the leader is one of spiritual maturity. Finally verse 7 reveals that a biblical leader should be "well thought of by outsiders." So putting it all together: a biblical leader should be a mature and disciplined believer who effectively leads his home, enjoys the affirmation of spiritual maturity by the congregation, and has a respected witness in the surrounding secular community. Think about it in reverse order: a leader cannot have a positive effect on the surrounding community without having the respect of his congregation. And the leader cannot be effective in the church without being effective within the family. All of this requires the vitality of personal spiritual gospel formation.

Here's an analogy that I remember from my first pastorate, which was in Miami. One evening I attended a meeting at a spectacular hotel in Miami Beach. It had a magnificent fountain in the lobby. Water rose from a reservoir and flowed into a small laver. From there, the water overflowed into another laver, then into another—and finally it flowed into a basin from which it was recycled. I've often thought of that fountain as a wonderful analogy of the work of grace in the life of a believer. The grace of Jesus Christ is propelled by the Holy Spirit (as he illuminates God's Word) into the believer's personal life; then—like the water flowing through the fountain's lavers—it overflows into the believer's family, then into the church, and finally into the community. At the heart of God's work in the believer, the family, the church, and the community is the influence of Bible-based leadership.

Now, you may have heard this set of priorities taught this way: Put God first, then family, church, work, community, and everything else. Is that biblical? Scripture certainly does emphasize putting God and others first before self, but I believe Scripture reveals a much more foundational approach to lifestyle prioritizing. God is not at the top of our priority list, he *is* our list. Therefore, he through his Word makes our priority list. Our Lord does not simply call us to put him first in life. The passion for the preeminence of Christ is a call to make him our life. "For to me to live is Christ . . ." (Phil. 1:21). We don't love God with most of our heart, mind, and soul but "with all of our heart, mind and soul." Believers' lives should be Christ-centered and Christ-consumed. As the lordship of Christ transforms us, the priorities of life will, of necessity, be established by him as our Lord. Personal formation, family formation, church participation, and community impact will be the result. Leaders show the way by their Christ-centered and Christ-consumed lives framed by Christ-given priorities as we live our lives fully and completely given to him. *Godliness is more important than giftedness.*

Finally, the fourth biblical requirement for leadership is: *Leaders are to be position-bearers, not position-wearers.* What's the difference? For the answer, examine 1 Timothy 3:1: "If anyone aspires to the office of overseer, he desires a noble task." Look at the text carefully.

It teaches that leadership is a *task*—a noble task indeed, but still a *task*. In other words, leadership is work. It's a call to commitment that requires physical, mental, emotional, and spiritual exercise and sacrifice. Christian leaders must be mature, disciplined, and respected because the pressures of leadership multiply the challenges of life. For instance, a leader must sometimes endure sustained or frequent attacks by sideline critics and skeptics, and still remain loving and focused. The leader also immediately goes into Satan's crosshairs. Satan wants to scatter the sheep by striking down the shepherd. Leadership is a call of love and passion, but it's also *work—hard work:* the work of a mature faith rooted in the sufficiency of Christ and growing in grace, maturing in leadership, and walking confidently and carefully for Christ.

Part of that work is protecting crucial personal lifestyle priorities. A leader must work effectively and diligently to prioritize time in God's Word and prayer, embrace the Sabbath, obtain rest, and sequester time with family, especially his spouse. And a leader's work and demands don't always conveniently fall into neat categories. Life is messy. And a leader is required to sacrificially wade into that messiness with the love and truth of Jesus Christ as a servant. That is why a leader must aspire to be a position-bearer, not a position-wearer. A genuine Christian leader doesn't accept a call to leadership in order to acquire a title, to expand a résumé, or to build a future obituary. Instead, a genuine leader exercises leadership to exalt the Lord and shepherd his family and the church while thoughtfully committing to influence the world for Christ and reproduce leaders who will shake the world.

Furthermore, the work of leadership is actually an act of worship, and we should embrace it with the same passion we are called to bring to the act of corporate worship. That's why Paul urged Timothy to "fulfill your ministry" (2 Tim. 4:5). The call to leadership is not a call to fulfill yourself but to fulfill the ministry. Paul's objective was not self-fulfillment but self-sacrifice for ministry fulfillment. This is why he declares before his death for Christ: "I am already being poured out as a drink offering" (2 Tim. 4:6). This was not a statement of self-congratulation but a declaration of thanksgiving to his God who had called him to life and leadership. Burnt offerings have ashes left. Drink offerings have nothing left. Paul had fulfilled his ministry by emptying himself to love and lead for Christ.

Three Traps to Avoid

Knowing that biblical leadership is a privilege, not an entitlement, and knowing that Satan especially targets leaders, we must avoid his traps. A Christian leader has been saved by grace like any other believer and is undergoing the God-ordained refining that every Christian experiences. Yet the privilege of Christian leadership can be forfeited if a leader engages in deliberate or scandalous behavior and is no longer above reproach. For example, three schemes of Satan that have entrapped countless Christian leaders are *indolence, immorality,* and *insubordination*. Upon these rocks many leaders have shipwrecked their lives, their families, their ministry, and their leadership.

Indolence

Indolence is nothing more than habitual laziness. Followers are dependent on leaders, and there's no room for habitual laziness in leadership. Certainly work must be measured and planned and must include rest and recreation, but a Christian leader should never be vulnerable to the accusation of laziness. The book of Proverbs teaches that laziness is the sign of an undisciplined, unmotivated lifestyle and does not glorify God. In contrast, the lifestyle of a genuine Christian leader is marked by industriousness. Scripture reveals that Jesus was never hurried or frenzied, yet he was always going "straightway" or "immediately" to the next divine appointment. His lifestyle was energetic but focused, and he properly sustained leadership activity with appropriate periods of physical and spiritual renewal and rest. An industrious leader is prepared for a crisis and its accompanying demands, and he doesn't contribute to it by carelessness or indolence. A genuine leader doesn't relish a crisis, but is prepared to meet it and will not be AWOL (Absent Without Leave) when the moment of crisis arrives.

Immorality

The most prevalent sin destroying Christian leaders today is probably immorality, especially sexual immorality. Many Christians in America today can list numerous leaders whose lives, families, and ministries have been wrecked or damaged by sexual immorality. Can a leader who falls to adultery or fornication be restored and reconciled in the home and in the church? Yes—sexual immorality is not the unforgivable sin. But it *is* extremely destructive to the element of trust that's so essential to leadership, and full restoration to authority will, of necessity, require much supervised time and effort. God's advice on this issue is powerfully simple and effective: *flee temptation.* Satan's assault is incessant. Contemporary American culture is a hypersexualized society that flaunts sexual impropriety, promiscuity, and perversion. So flee temptation. Don't try to resist it—*flee it.* "Blessed is the man who remains steadfast under trial, for when he has stood the test he will receive the crown of life, which God has promised to those who love him. Let no one say when he is tempted, 'I am being tempted by God,' for God cannot be tempted with evil, and he himself tempts no one. But each person is tempted when he is lured and enticed by his own desire. Then desire when it has conceived gives birth to sin, and sin when it is fully grown brings forth death" (James 1:12–15). How do you flee temptation? It's simple in most cases: always avoid putting yourself in harm's way. Flee all occasions to be tempted. Leaders should make a covenant with the Lord committing to sexual purity before marriage and sexual faithfulness within marriage. As part of your covenant before God, guard your eyes, your thoughts, and your conversation in order to effectively guard your actions. Christian leaders should honor God's ordinance of marriage by remaining sexually pure before marriage, continuing to be pure during marriage, and joyfully exercising God-created sexual love within marriage.

A practical defensive weapon in this age is an accountability partner or group. For almost twenty-five years, I have been blessed by the redemptive relationship of an accountability group. It's my "band of brothers." Each of us has made a vow that if one of us appears to falter in the area of sexual immorality, the others will hold him accountable and will help restore him back into a walk with the Lord, the church, and most of all his family and marriage. At the same time, we have agreed to collectively insist that if any of us succumbs to sexual immorality by violating our marriage covenant, he must leave the pastoral ministry. For us, the door to leadership and ministry swings open one way and only one time. We didn't make this agreement because we presume to possess exceptional character—quite the opposite. We hold each other accountable because we fully understand our inherent sinfulness and our ever-present weaknesses. Therefore, if or when we are tempted to engage in sexual unfaithfulness, we must admit to ourselves: *This will bring shame on the Lord's name and it will cost me my ministry. Is it worth it?* By establishing a structure of accountability, we are striving to flee temptation before it even occurs. We call all of our agreed accountabilities "obstacles to sin" and "stepping stones to obedience."

Insubordination

The final failure that can disqualify a leader is insubordination. The Bible is powerfully frank on this subject: it demands that all believers and all churches embrace the doctrine of submission. If a leader cannot submit to others, he is unprepared to lead anyone. Ephesians 5:21 commands, "Submit to one another out of reverence for Christ" (NIV). This means that both Christians and churches are to be in submission to one another. Hebrews 13:17 says, "Obey your leaders and submit to them." Church members must submit to leaders, and leaders must submit to those in authority over them. If you yourself cannot submit, you should not expect others to submit to you. In fact, leaders must intentionally exhibit a lifestyle of submission to those in authority over them. The privilege of leadership does not elevate the leader above submission; instead, it calls the leader to be a model of submission. There is no such thing as an independent Christian or an independent leader. One crucial way in which our dependence on the Lord is manifested is by submitting to one another. If a leader displays habitual insubordination rather than habitual submission, he is biblically unqualified for leadership.

So a biblical leader rejects indolence, immorality, and insubordination while seeking to live a grace-driven and Christ-centered life, which requires wisdom and accountability and a desire to be above reproach in his personal life, family life, church, and community. That's the profile of a biblically qualified leader—one who is called by the Lord and prepared by the gospel for effective Christian leadership. *An overseer must be above reproach.*

If Scripture defines the leader, then would not God's Word also define leadership? Absolutely. Now it's time to discover what the profile of biblical leadership is so that we can develop the leaders that have been defined in God's Word and then deploy them not only throughout the church but into the world. The world is in desperate need of these leadership change agents who will once again turn the world upside down, which would, in fact, turn the world back to right side up. So, what does world-shaking leadership look like?

6

WHAT *IS* LEADERSHIP?

"But seek first the kingdom of God and his righteousness,
and all these things will be added to you."
MATTHEW 6:33

Ronald Reagan was very controversial.

Today we often hear about our fortieth president's political wisdom and personal fortitude from both sides of the political aisle. But if you're old enough to have lived during Ronald Reagan's two-term presidency, you probably remember how unpopular he was in some circles, especially for denouncing Communism. When he took office, the United States was at the high point of a period of appeasement with the old Soviet Union. It was a well-intentioned but obviously naïve approach— pretending that the Soviets really didn't want to take over the world and install totalitarian Communism everywhere while we basically begged them to play nice. But it didn't work. Instead of respecting the autonomy of other nations and granting freedom to the Eastern European nations they already suppressed, the Soviet leadership promoted the violent communist takeover of one nation after another: Afghanistan, Angola, Mozambique, Nicaragua, Grenada.

As the new president of the United States, Ronald Reagan repeatedly offered to negotiate with the Soviets, but only from a position of American strength. His policy was trust and verify. He believed that Communism was morally bankrupt and therefore could not be trusted and verification was needed. He also believed that Communism would implode if America stood firm for freedom. He built up the U.S. military from a state of decline, called for freedom for all people oppressed by Communism, and courageously called on the Soviet leadership to renounce what he called their "evil empire." He clearly stated his position to a 1983 convention of the National Association of Evangelicals: "Yes, let us pray for the salvation of all of those who live in that totalitarian darkness—pray they will discover the joy of knowing God. But until they do, let us be aware that while they preach the supremacy of the state, declare its omnipotence over individual man, and predict its eventual domination of all peoples on the Earth, they are the focus of evil in the modern world."[1]

Many American politicians, academics, members of the news media, and others were really upset by Reagan's words. This affable, easygoing American leader became extremely controversial. Newspaper editors, television commentators, political opponents, foreign leaders, and others were harshly critical of him. They ridiculed his policy, his intelligence, his character, his age, and even his hair. But he proved them all wrong. Eventually the communist Soviet Union collapsed, unable to match Reagan's defense buildup, unable to disprove his "evil empire" accusation, and unable to repress the desire for freedom from the millions within its sphere—including countless Christians. Led by Ronald Reagan, the United States won the Cold War. *Leadership* works. Good leadership produces good results and bad leadership produces bad results. Jesus affirms this when he says, "It is enough for the disciple to be like his teacher, and the servant like his master" (Matt. 10:25) and "if the blind lead the blind, both will fall into a pit" (Matt. 15:14). Since leadership works, to get good results we need to define, develop, and deploy good leaders.

Ronald Wilson Reagan was overall a good leader. If you had told those of us who were growing up in the 1960s that the Berlin Wall would be torn down and Communism would collapse in on itself, we would have dismissed you as at best naïve and possibly insane. Reagan saw what needed to happen, what could happen, and how it needed to happen, and he led the way. Now what are the maxims that guide good leaders who transform the landscape of the future?

Three Maxims of Effective Leadership

Great Leaders Know Their Mission and Are Unalterably Committed to Achieving It

How did Reagan do it? And how did he remain unwavering under such a harsh and prolonged assault by his own countrymen? The answer: he knew his mission; he was steadfastly committed to achieving it; he refused to be paralyzed by fear; and without hesitation he would communicate the mission with passion and initiate the strategy for its success. Of much greater significance for Christian leaders is Christ as a leader who was unalterably committed to achieving his mission. He came into this world on a mission to save sinners, defeat Satan, and win the victory for his church. He allowed nothing to deter him. The dread of the cup of suffering that he would drink, the awesomeness of the challenge in facing death, sin, hell, and the grave, and even his "descent into hell" and separation from his Father would not keep him from achieving his mission for the glory of his Father. To some measure it is that leadership focus and passion which consumes Christian leaders who are following Christ, their Lord and Savior. Great leadership requires understanding the mission and holding to an unyielding commitment to remain faithful to it. Neither self-promotion, nor self-preservation, nor pride, nor fear, nor weariness should deter a leader from faithfully fulfilling the mission. For the Christian leader, our marching orders are both simple and profound. First, we are called to personally "seek first the kingdom of God and his righteousness, and all these things will be added to you" (Matt. 6:33). Second, as Christian leaders we are committed to continually reproduce ourselves by making disciples who are Christ-centered and bring an unquenchable passion for "the preeminence of Christ in all things." Finally, we execute our specific responsibilities as a Christian leader in the task, initiative, or organization that has been entrusted to us.

Great Leaders Take Care of Their People

One of the greatest moments in the life of Jesus that inspires and instructs us is his intercessory prayer before he goes to the cross (recorded in John 17). He makes seven requests; one of them is for the protection of his followers after his atoning death, which aligns with his vigilant care throughout his life ministry in discipling them. "I do not ask that you take them out of the world, but that you protect them from the evil one" (John 17:15). And which one of us is not aware of the famous lesson from the allegory of the good shepherd? We are challenged in our leadership by the reminder of Christ's commitment to lay down his life for the sheep. Furthermore, he states in the Scripture that if one sheep wanders he will pursue it. Christ takes care of his people. The great challenge is knowing how to care for people and lead them against Satan, when you know they are called to be engaged in spiritual warfare and are therefore under Satan's assault. Here is one example:

Omar Bradley was one of the greatest American military commanders of World War II. He was a gifted strategist, able to foresee what the enemy might do and able to develop a winning battle plan—but that's not what made him great. He was a competent tactician, able to effectively execute orders and bring forces to bear in an efficient manner—but that's not what made him great. He was superb at the operational arts and was able to direct complicated operations, motivate subordinates, support his superiors, and cooperate with his peer officers—but that's not what made him great. As a career army officer and a West

Pointer, Bradley was disappointed to have missed a field command in World War I; he was kept busy training troops until war's end. When World War II began, he chafed for a combat command, but he dutifully accepted one stateside command after another, training troops. Eventually, he earned his combat command, rose to field commander of Operation Overlord—the D-Day invasion of Normandy—and wound up commanding more troops than any other field commander in American history. But even that's not what made him great, trusted, admired, and loved.

Before being called to combat, Bradley was placed in command of training the U.S. Army's Eighty-second and Twenty-eighth Infantry Divisions—huge bodies of troops who would be placed at the heart of the American war effort in the war's European theater. Bradley approached his command with commendable zeal and with determination that his troops would be both motivated and protected as much as possible. To accomplish that goal, he made sure that all arriving recruits were welcomed to camp by a military band to boost morale. When they marched to their barracks, they found awaiting them new uniforms, the best equipment available, and a hot meal. Bradley also implemented a demanding physical training program, which prepared the citizen-soldiers of World War II for life in the field. His men loved him for it, fought long and hard in response, and kept lifelong respect and affection for General Bradley.

Other successful American commanders of World War II— General George Patton, for instance—achieved battlefield fame, but only Omar Bradley left a legacy as "the soldier's general." How did he do it? By excelling at the number-two maxim of great leadership: *great leaders take care of their people.* Not only do great leaders resolutely commit to achieving the mission, but they always strive to do the best for those who serve under them and are in their care.

Great Leaders Intentionally Produce Leaders

In November 1965, Lieutenant Colonel Harold "Hal" Moore Jr. and the U.S. Seventh Cavalry's First Battalion were engaged in one of the opening battles of the Vietnam War. Surrounded by an estimated 4,000 North Vietnamese regulars at a jungle clearing called Landing Zone X-Ray, Moore's 450 soldiers were taking searing fire from all sides. Even with crucial American air support, his outnumbered troops faced annihilation. Moore was determined that his men would survive, however, and he directed a heroic defense in what proved to be one of the fiercest battles of the war. He and his soldiers repulsed repeated assaults and inflicted severe casualties on the enemy until his battalion was finally relieved by reinforcements. The dramatic story is told in the 1992 best seller, *We Were Soldiers Once . . . and Young,* which was made into an acclaimed motion picture.[2]

Moore won the army's highest award, the Distinguished Service Cross, and eventually rose to the rank of lieutenant general. He was renowned for his superb leadership skills. A scene in the movie captured his foresight and grasp of leadership principles when Moore's character confronted a squad leader who had been unceremoniously "killed" in a training exercise. "You are dead," Moore declared. "Now, who do you have ready to take your place?" The scene reflects both the reality of warfare and a key element of leadership—the third maxim: *great leaders always prepare to reproduce and multiply themselves.*

That's one of the main responsibilities of a great leader: being prepared to reproduce and multiply leadership. In military warfare, a leader is always a target, and it's no different in spiritual warfare. Remember, Satan always has leaders in his crosshairs. Salvation is free. Discipleship costs. Leadership costs a lot more. There is always a price to pay in leadership, a principle affirmed in Zechariah 13:7: "Strike the shepherd, and the sheep will be scattered." The Bible teaches that we Christians strive against the world, the flesh, and the devil—and all three forces incessantly attack leadership. The world, especially contemporary American culture, instinctively rebels against all expressions of biblical leadership. Our own flesh tempts us to shrink back in fear, strike out in anger, accommodate in appeasement, or isolate ourselves with legalism. And of course, Satan is on the prowl for ways to attack Christian leaders at every opportunity. Jesus warned Peter (and us) that God's leaders are Satan's targets. "Simon, Simon," he is recorded as saying, "behold, Satan demanded to have you [plural], that he might sift you [plural] like wheat, but I have prayed for you [singular] that your faith may not fail" (Luke 22:31–32). Remember, Satan "prays" against leaders and Satan "preys" on leaders. Jesus has allowed us to see that Satan's design at that moment was to eradicate all twelve leaders, and even though they faltered at the moment of trial, the Lord brought them back. And, if extra-biblical historical accounts are correct, they ultimately gave themselves as martyrs in serving Christ, obviously no longer controlled by fear. Judas was lost in his treason and unrepentant desolation. Peter denied Christ three times. Judas died in suicidal despair, but Peter was reclaimed and restored and became a great leader. What was the difference between Peter and Judas? The intercession of Christ: "I have prayed for you" (Luke 22:32). Praise the Lord, he ever lives and "is interceding for us" (Rom. 8:34).

Knowing that fighting the good fight requires a multitude of leaders and realizing that leaders sometimes become casualties, Christian leaders must intentionally reproduce themselves and multiply. Some leaders are casualties by divine appointment, and unfortunately some are casualties by carelessness. But eventually all of us will be called home. Who will be there to take our place? Paul had Timothy and others prepared to replace him. Elijah prepared Elisha. Moses prepared Joshua and Caleb. Jesus, our great leader, had the Seventy, the Twelve, and the Three prepared when he ascended to heaven. A Christian leader's finishing line might be God's call to come home at the appointed end of a ministry or it might be on the field of battle. Christian leadership therefore requires a commitment to reproduction and multiplication. Great leaders strive to do both. By making such preparation, they leave behind not a vacuum or a vacancy waiting to be filled by false leaders produced by the world, but instead, they leave behind ready replacements who have been nurtured and discipled by gospel leaders to expand the kingdom of God throughout this world.

This crucial maxim once prompted a memorable conversation with my son. As he neared graduation from college, I shared some family history that I hoped would make a point. I admitted to my son that I had failed as his father at times, and I asked him to forgive me. Then I explained to him that despite my failings, he had been given a better father than I had been given. I quickly explained that the same had been true for me—I had been given a better father than my dad had been given. And his father, who was my grandfather, had been a better father than the father he had been given. I knew this from the legacy of spiritual growth in our family. It wasn't that some in our family line were greater sinners than others; it was a fact of Christian discipleship and God's faithfulness within a covenant family. That's the way it should be, I told my son: those who follow in a line of believers should always take spiritual maturity to a higher level than those who came before him. That's what good discipleship and effective leadership will produce. By the grace of God and the proper exercise of disciplined leadership, my son and daughters will take this spiritual legacy to a new level of spiritual growth and maturity in Christ and for Christ. Therefore, our family will continue to be blessed by the truth of Psalm 16:6: "The lines have fallen for me in pleasant places; indeed, I have a beautiful inheritance."

The church as the family of God must be committed to the reproduction and multiplication of leadership. One of the reasons the church falters in the next generation is because we do not pass on the legacy of Christian leadership and fail to disciple effective leaders who can take the church and its mission forward to extend the kingdom of God to the next level in the next generation. The result of allowing a vacuum of leadership is that Satan will quickly fill the vacuum not only in the world but also in the church with false leaders who will propagate the devolution of the culture and create a death spiral. Leaders who do not follow this biblical principle are failing, and those who humbly seek to be God's great leaders will remain ever mindful of this crucial component as well as the other maxims of leadership. The test of great leaders is not the *size* of their followership but that they attract and intentionally develop the next generation of leaders. *Great leaders intentionally reproduce themselves.*

Failures to Avoid

These three maxims—*great leaders know their mission and are unalterably committed to achieving it; great leaders take care of their people; great leaders intentionally reproduce leaders*—seem so obvious upon reflection. So why are they so often ignored or neglected? The answer is clear: distraction and destruction potentially loom before every existing leader. To avoid distraction and destruction every leader must beware of Satan's designed traps. What are they?

Failure to Keep the Main Thing as the Main Thing. A salesman was riding along the interstate highway. In the field he saw a young boy with a bow and arrow standing beside a barn, which had numerous arrows stuck in the bull's-eye of numerous targets. The salesman stopped to watch this presumably expert archer. The young man strung the bow and launched another arrow into the side of the barn. He then approached the barn, picked up a bucket of paint and a paint brush, and proceeded to paint a target around the arrow. That moment reflects the leadership style of many leaders today. We shoot multiple arrows of activity but have no target. When we are through we declare our activity as the target. Do you know your target—your mission—and is it faithful to God's Word and your calling? If so, do you maintain the personal discipline to keep it as a priority? Every need is not your call: are you spread too thin on too many fronts to effectively fulfill your God-given mission? Don't be distracted by momentary fascinations and fads. Don't be diverted by prolonged "emergencies." Don't be detoured by the tyranny of what others declare as urgent. Don't be impulsive; instead be

71

thoughtfully and prayerfully deliberate. Be responsive, but do not be easily detoured. Don't let even good things obscure the important things. More than one gifted ministry leader has lost sight of the defined mission by becoming repeatedly enamored by every possibility or fascinated by someone else's leadership or distracted by unrelated issues or even lured by opportunities for personal acclaim and advancement. Following such "leadership" is like being in a car with a sixteen-year-old who has not learned how to drive properly. The vehicle careens from one side of the lane to the other, erratically increases speed, suddenly brakes to a halt, then zooms forward again. The passengers in this driver's care become unnerved, exhausted, and hopeless of ever experiencing a steady ride. Eventually, they will abandon either the vehicle or its driver, and much time and distance is lost. Keep the main thing as the main thing! The God-given mission for the leader must be guarded as sacred, and the leader must both embrace it and be absorbed with it. God establishes the target for the leader. The leader then, as God's called servant leader, must be obsessed with target fixation.

Failure to Maintain the Integrity of the Message. Failure also follows when a Christian leader forsakes the integrity of the God-given message and content of the mission. Don't become a pragmatist, convincing yourself that the end justifies the means—or massaging and editing the message. All scriptural doctrines are important. Some are primary, some are secondary, and some are tertiary. In the primary and essential teaching of Scripture we must be clear and unyielding. In secondary and tertiary teaching we must give charity as people grapple with these important doctrines, realizing they are not essential in terms of salvation. Yet, we must also realize that they are not unimportant. Learn to major on the majors and minor on the minors. That doesn't mean compromise, but it does mean being patient, charitable, and respectful when dealing with secondary and tertiary biblical issues. For instance, baptism is important but it is not necessary for salvation. Therefore, while realizing that there is a biblical position on the subject, because it is nonessential for salvation, we have the liberty to be patient with one another as we work through the issue. But, we must also realize that Christian leaders can make primary errors in how they deal with secondary doctrines. Sometimes it is tempting to place peace before purity. Don't compromise the integrity of the biblical message to fulfill your mission.

Great leaders know how to stay both on mission and on message at the same time. Is it easy in today's culture? No, of course not. It requires knowledge of the Word, fidelity to the message, commitment to the mission, and humble reliance on the grace of God while treating others with respect and dignity. Yet remember that the Great Commission, which directs every Christian leader, requires us to teach all that he has commanded in his Word. The apostle Paul declared he was innocent of the blood of all men (Acts 20:26) because he had publicly and privately with tears declared to them the whole counsel of God. It is crucial to teach all of God's Word, yet to begin with the essential and primary doctrines. Yet in the name of pursuing success and effectiveness, we cannot dismiss secondary and tertiary doctrines from God's Word and still fulfill our mission.

Fear of Failure. It's easy to identify leaders who are governed by fear of failure. They become indecisive or hesitant, or they even attempt to pass decisions or responsibilities on to others. A question that I enjoy asking when interviewing someone for a leadership position is, will you please identify three instances in which you've failed and what you've learned from each failure? It's a revealing question for a leader. If you've never experienced a failure, you've never exercised leadership. An absence of failure usually reflects an unwillingness to take risks because of a fear of failure. Great leaders do not "play safe." Leadership requires risks. Of course, a ministry replete with continual failures reflects other problems, and a responsible leader is not rash or impetuous. A humble willingness to be decisive and aggressive—prayerfully and thoughtfully—is inherent to leadership, and sometimes it results in failure. A great leader then seizes that moment for personal development, turning the experience into an instructive failure. If you have a debilitating fear of failure, surrender it to the Lord and ask him for courage to lead others forward in a responsible manner with your confidence in the strength and might of your God. Thomas J. "Stonewall" Jackson, a noted and aggressive general in the Civil War, collected maxims. One of his most used was, "Never take counsel from your fears." In other words, never plan out of fear.

Failure to Take Care of Yourself. Leaders fail when they neglect caring for themselves. "Pay close attention to yourself and to your teaching," Paul admonished Timothy (1 Tim. 4:16, NASB). "Discipline yourself for the purpose of godliness" (1 Tim. 4:7, NASB); "be strong in the grace that is in Christ Jesus" (2 Tim. 2:1, NASB). Leaders cannot focus on their mission, care for their people, or reproduce and multiply if they do not take care of themselves. Spiritual care is the first priority. Practice what you preach. Do not neglect a regular time with the Lord in prayer and the Word. Ministry preparation—preaching, teaching, serving—is not the same as personal time with the Lord. Nourish yourself spiritually. Don't neglect to confess your sins and receive the blessing and empowerment of God's forgiveness. Avoid compromise, violating your conscience, and falling into patterns of sin. Maintain your witness with a faithful lifestyle. Strive before the Lord to live above reproach to honor your Savior.

Also, take care of yourself physically and emotionally. "You shall not put the Lord your God to the test," as we're reminded in Matthew 4:7 (quoting Deut. 6:16). As a leader, you're required to care for your body as the Lord's temple just as everyone else must. Follow a healthful diet. Exercise. Plan free personal time in your schedule. Spend time with your family, enjoy a hobby, get a healthful amount of sleep, avoid stress. Do what's right and necessary to take care of yourself. Remember, the Christian life and Christian leadership is not a sprint—it's a marathon.

Pace yourself so you can finish strong physically, emotionally, and spiritually.

Failure to Learn Lessons or Receive Discipline. Finally, leaders fail when they become prideful or arrogant. Show me a leader who refuses to learn from his mistakes or who refuses to humbly accept discipline, and I will show you a leader who is racing toward failure. You cannot lead others if you yourself are unwilling to be led or unwilling to learn. Often, our greatest learning experiences come through our failures—and a leader must be willing to humbly admit error and learn from it. Sometimes we must receive discipline from our peers or our superiors. Many times in life we *will* be disciplined by the Lord. This is how we grow, and it is a gift of God's grace.

Remember this admonition:

> "My son, do not regard lightly the discipline of the Lord,
>   nor be weary when reproved by him.
> For the Lord disciplines the one he loves,
>   and chastises every son whom he receives. . . ."
>
> For the moment all discipline seems painful rather than pleasant, but later it yields the peaceful fruit of righteousness to those who have been trained by it. (Heb. 12:5–6, 11; quoting Prov. 3:11–12)

The Christian leader needs to enjoy the grace of the Lord Jesus through surrendering to the Holy Spirit and keeping the heart and lifestyle of a learner. The joyful learner will invariably exhibit a voracious appetite to continually grow in the Lord and to be a leader who leads by example. So remember, Christian, in this dark new age: keep the main thing as the main thing. Maintain the integrity of the message. Surrender any fear of failure. Take care of yourself. And be willing to keep learning, even from discipline. As you do this, you will avoid the classic temptations that regularly bring down neglectful leaders. Remember that leadership begins by following these three maxims: *Great leaders know their mission and are unalterably committed to achieving it. Great leaders take care of their people. Great leaders intentionally produce leaders.* This is why, when a leader shows up, things change. Now let's see how and why things change and make sure they change for the better and for the glory of our triune God.

7

THERMOMETER OR THERMOSTAT?

"A worker who has no need to be ashamed."
2 TIMOTHY 2:15

Turn on the TV. Pick up a newspaper. Listen to the radio. Do an Internet search for any subject.

You'll quickly realize that American leadership is increasingly composed of "thermometer leaders," not "thermostat leaders." A thermometer has one use: to sense and then communicate the room temperature. A thermostat, on the other hand, is used to change the temperature. A thermostat will measure the temperature of a room and then adjust it as needed. As contemporary American culture continues its death spiral, thermostat leaders are desperately needed—leaders who will help transform the culture from death to life. But while we have few thermostat leaders, we're inundated with legions of thermometer leaders.

They're everywhere—in politics, education, arts, and sadly, even the church. They reflect our declining culture by absorbing its fascination with and addiction to greed, sexual immorality, consumerism, narcissism, and self-promotion. They propagate the culture of death in a variety of ways: abortion, euthanasia, drugs, sexual promiscuity, and violence. But what if the church began *defining, developing,* and *deploying* thermostat leaders? Leaders in every state. Every city. Every town. Every church. Would our world change? No doubt—the only question is how and how quickly.

Three Thermostat Leaders

The old adage is true: one person *can* make a difference and, if committed to the Lord, a significant difference. "O Lord, I want to know about you," a man named George once called out. "I want to know about your creation. O God, I want to know about the universe." He sensed that the Lord answered his prayer with a negative: "No, George, the universe is too big for you." He conceded that truth, but prayed again. "All right, Lord," he said, "if not the universe, tell me all about the earth." "But George," he sensed the Lord telling him, "that is still too big for you." Another no. Exasperated, he cried out, "God, I want to help my people." Then he dramatically lowered his goal. "Teach me about a peanut for your glory," he prayed.

And God did. George—an extraordinary chemist, educator, artist, and agriculturalist—transformed the South and affected the entire nation because he was humble enough to submit his will to God's. He also became internationally famous as George Washington Carver, the prodigious inventor of the many uses of the tiny peanut. One of my prized possessions is a picture in my study of him working in a modest laboratory at Tuskegee University. Carver identified more than three hundred uses for the lowly Southern peanut—from peanut butter to cosmetics—and more than a hundred uses for the sweet potato. His commitment was not without distractions—some quite flattering and tempting. The acclaimed scientist Thomas Edison offered him a prestigious job with a huge salary. So did pioneer automaker Henry Ford. Carver declined both. Why did George Washington Carver turn down both of these offers, which were reported to be over $100,000?

Because he wanted to be faithful to the Lord's call upon his life, which was more important than personal advancement, acclaim, or affluence. It wasn't about money or fame. His calling was to help lift the people of the South from agricultural and economic ruin, and to help prepare the first generation of freed slaves for a new life—and his approach was intentionally based on biblical principles. So George Washington Carver turned away from fame and fortune, and for a salary of $1,500 a year, he teamed up with another former slave, Booker T. Washington, to establish Alabama's Tuskegee University. For George Washington Carver, it wasn't about money. It wasn't about fame. It was about obedience—to the Lord and to his calling. The result was a legacy educational institution, a rescued and transformed society, and a leadership model that is still affecting our culture. That's thermostat leadership.

George Washington Carver's love for the Lord and his drive to serve were matched in kind by his colleague, Booker T. Washington. *His* calling? He was determined to educate a generation of former slaves and their children, and he did so from a biblically based perspective. He believed former slaves and their offspring were not a burden to American society, but instead constituted an untapped asset. Both men believed that an emphasis on Christian education and character could enable those who had been on the bottom rung of society to become genuine achievers and productive citizens. Booker T. Washington was not waiting for someone to give him and this newly emancipated generation of African-Americans a seat at the table. He had a vision that his people would make the table and sell the table, and that their character and conduct would of necessity create a desire to invite his students to the table as honored guests. Not only did he believe that—he accomplished it personally. It wasn't easy for a black American to take a public position in those days, but Washington followed his calling, turning down multiple lucrative offers. That's thermostat leadership.

Speaking of being invited to a table as an honored guest, Booker T. Washington so impressed President Theodore Roosevelt that

"Teddy" invited him to the White House. That momentous event was the first time an African-American had ever been honored to sit at the table of a White House luncheon. It was a bold and courageous act of leadership by Roosevelt. News of the event sparked a media outcry, but the former Rough Rider was undeterred, and afterward developed a friendship with Washington. Roosevelt made Booker T. Washington an influential member of his unofficial circle of advisers—his "kitchen cabinet"—and turned to him for advice on securing qualified leadership to make appointments in the South. It was an important precedent for the nation, and Roosevelt needed sacrificial courage to do it. That's thermostat leadership. None of these three men—Carver, Washington, or Roosevelt—was a thermometer leader, playing it safe and fitting into the culture. They were thermostat leaders; they were leaders with integrity, and fulfilling their mission and calling was the result. Our nation was changed for the better, and we are still being blessed by them to this day. All three men were Christians, and like other Christian leaders in the Bible and history they manifested three qualities necessary to be a thermostat leader.

Three Essential Qualities of Thermostat Leadership

Determined, focused, and principled leadership refuses to be narcissistic, self-promotional, or greed-driven. Instead, it seeks to be faithful to the Lord and serve others, and in doing so, it can change the landscape of life. But how can we develop such leaders and what is the curriculum for their formation? One day while reading Hebrews 13:7, which could be characterized as a "followership" verse, I was struck not only by the marvelous exhortation to followers but the embedded presuppositions about leaders whom Christians should follow. "Remember your leaders, those who spoke to you the word of God. Consider the outcome of their way of life, imitate their faith." Clearly the text is exhorting followers to remember their leaders, follow them, listen to them, and imitate them. But notice the three assumptions about these Christian leaders. First, their *character* and conduct was worthy of imitation by their followers. Second, they could speak the Word of God because they knew the Word of God, since you cannot teach what you do not know. They were leaders of *content*. Third, they were able to lead, so obviously they had leadership *competencies*. These three elements are embedded in Scripture as essential to the development of principle-driven, influential thermostat leaders: *character, content,* and *competency*.

Character

Leaders whom we are to imitate must have lives worthy of imitation, therefore a Christian leader must have godly *character*. It's the foundation of the other two elements. Leadership content and competencies are meaningless without it. Unfortunately, I have seen ministry leaders who are theologically knowledgeable (content) and/or personally charismatic and effective (competent) destroy churches and organizations because of a lack of Christian character. Godly character is driven by the grace of God, focused on the glory of God, empowered by the Spirit of God, and defined by the Word of God—all the while propelled by the love of God. Character counts.

Circumstances do not determine your character, they reveal it, and become the occasion to refine it.

Here's a classic example:

General Robert E. Lee, a devout believer who felt compelled to defend his state in the Civil War even though he opposed secession and despised slavery, was left with practically nothing but hardship when the war ended. His home, Arlington Plantation, which overlooked Washington, D.C., from the Virginia side of the Potomac River, had been confiscated by the federal government and turned into a military cemetery. His wife had become an invalid. One of his daughters had died. He had suffered a series of heart attacks that left him in questionable health, and he had no foreseeable income. A prominent insurance company offered him a huge salary simply for the use of his name as an endorsement, but Lee declined, replying that his fame as a military commander had come at the cost of many soldiers' lives and he would not take advantage of them. Furthermore, Robert E. Lee explained, "my name is not for sale at any price."[1] I often think of that whenever I encounter a mindless celebrity product endorsement. Instead, he accepted a comparatively small salary of $1,500 a year as president of Washington College—now Washington and Lee University—a small, obscure Southern college in Virginia's Shenandoah Valley. There, he committed himself to instilling young people with a character-based education rooted in Christian ethics, which he believed could help restore a broken nation. Meanwhile, he sought to set a personal example of reconciliation and reunion.

Lee's character made him a success in his peacetime calling and earned him the respect of the entire nation—North and South—and it was demonstrated on multiple occasions even before he took the job at Washington College. After he surrendered his army at Appomattox in April 1865, signaling to all other Southern commanders that the war was over, Lee returned to his wartime home in Richmond. He worshiped each Lord's Day at St. Paul's Protestant Episcopal Church, pushing his wife to worship in a wheelchair. Worship services at St. Paul's were racially integrated, but the seating was segregated, with white worshipers seated on the ground floor and black worshipers seated in the church balcony. Sunday worship ended in communion, and the practice was for each group to sing hymns while the other group took communion—black worshipers singing while white worshipers were administered the Lord's Supper, then whites singing while blacks partook of the table.

Richmond was occupied by Northern troops at the time, and one June Sunday in 1865 two Northern soldiers attended worship to make sure that the pastor prayed publicly for the president of the United States—which he did. They also had another purpose in mind. When time came for communion to be administered, the two soldiers came forward leading a former African-American slave, obviously intending to evoke an incident. As they led the black man to kneel at the communion rail, the entire congregation—white and black—froze in place. A tense silence gripped the congregation. No one knew what to do until Robert E. Lee rose from his seat, walked with measured military cadence down the marble-floored aisle, knelt beside the black man, and put his hand on his shoulder. Then the two—black and white—were administered communion together by the pastor. Afterward, the entire congregation came forward from both floors and received the Lord's Supper on a glorious day in the life of St. Paul's Church. Several worshipers recorded the incident in their personal journals. What could have been a disastrous confrontation was transformed on that day into a celebration of the love of Christ regardless of race—all because of the Christ-centered character of one man.

Circumstances do not dictate character, but reveal it and become the occasion to refine it.

Content

The second essential element in developing a thermostat leader is *content*—a knowledgeable sound, biblical theology. Too many church leaders today have adopted a "cafeteria theology"—picking a little of what they like here and a little more there and ignoring the rest. A Christian leader cannot do that, but instead must embrace a theology that respects the Word of God as a "verbal, plenary inspiration"—fully inerrant right down to the choice and order of the Holy Spirit–inspired words. Sound theology requires us to frame everything by the Word of God—to consistently display a biblical worldview, to look at everything through the spectacles of God's Word. To live it, we must know it. To know it, we must study it. That's why 2 Timothy 2:15 commands each of us Christians, including leaders, to become "a worker who has no need to be ashamed, rightly handling the word of truth."

Genuine Christian leadership therefore begins with the leader's having assurance of personal salvation—that he or she has received Jesus Christ as Lord and Savior. A genuine Christian leader accepts the Word of God from Genesis through Revelation as inerrant in its original autographs, life-changing in practice, and authoritative as well as transformational over any and all human endeavors. A genuine Christian leader has a heart that is surrendered to live for the Lord and pursues a growing, consistent lifestyle that displays the evidence of salvation and a maturing walk with the Lord. Spiritual warfare for such a leader is inevitable. Satan will continually seek to undermine the character of Christians, especially leaders, with temptations to indolence, immorality, and insubordination. We flee Satan's temptations and we stand firm by *knowing* and *obeying* the Word of God in order to put on the "armor of God" (Eph. 6:11) while making full use of the "weapons of God" (2 Cor. 10:3–6).

Here is a list of some key areas of theology and Bible content that need to be incorporated in the development of a Christian leader:

- The doctrine of Scripture
- The doctrine of God
- The doctrine of man (in creation, fall, and redemption)
- The gospel
- The doctrines of church, state, family, etc.

Crucial to a sound theology is reliance on the biblical doctrine of divine providence. This essential biblical truth is succinctly stated in Romans 8:28: "And we know that for those who love God all things work together for good, for those who are called according to his purpose." Behind this doctrine is the loving smile of the Sovereign God. He does not promise that everything that comes into our lives as believers in this sinful world will be good, but that he will personally work all things together for our good. Trusting in the sovereignty of God enables a leader to avoid self-adulation and exaltation, to instead give glory to God in victory, knowing that it came from the hand of the Lord. In defeat, the leader is kept from the pit of despair because he knows that God is also at work in the adversities of life. Accepting the doctrine of divine providence is crucial to leadership. Praising God in victory and trusting him in the hard times of life enables a leader, and every other Christian, to grow in confidence and contentment. From this acceptance of divine providence comes God's grace, blessing believers with stability and peace, removing anxieties and fears, shielding us from self-centeredness, and enabling us to glorify God alone. Here is an example—again from the Civil War—of how trusting in the sovereignty of a providential God brings peace that indeed surpasses all understanding so that one's Christian character remains steadfast in the midst of any and all circumstances.

When he was shot down in the 1864 assault at Petersburg, thirty-five-year-old Colonel Joshua Lawrence Chamberlain was already a war hero. By vocation he was a teacher, a professor of theology and rhetoric at Maine's Bowdoin College, but he had left the classroom to join the Northern war effort as a volunteer officer in the Twentieth Maine Infantry. He proved to be a natural leader, survived some of the war's worst fighting at Antietam and Fredericksburg, and was promoted to colonel and commander of the regiment in time for the battle of Gettysburg. There, Chamberlain's leadership and command decisions helped save the battle for Northern forces, and eventually led him to be known throughout the North as the "hero of Gettysburg."

A year later, while commanding a brigade of federal troops at the siege of Petersburg, he was ordered to lead his brigade in a desperate assault against the Confederate line. Some officers believed it was a foolish order and a hopeless assignment: the assault route lay across a broad, open killing field, and massed fire from the Southern lines had already felled countless Northern troops. "My heart dropped to my shoes" when the order was issued, one of Chamberlain's fellow officers later recalled.[2] Despite the deadly odds, Chamberlain courageously led his troops forward. They were immediately struck by a searing torrent of enemy fire. The assault disintegrated, and Chamberlain, still holding his sword and the colors of his battalion, was shot down at the head of his troops. Dragged out of the line of fire by his men, he was carried to a field hospital. Army surgeons tried to save his life, but finally concluded that his case was hopeless. Nothing else could be done, they told the young officer, explaining that he would soon die. A devout Christian, Chamberlain asked for a scrap of paper and a pencil, and wrote a goodbye note to his wife back home in Maine:

> My darling wife
>   I am lying mortally wounded the doctors think, but my mind & heart are at peace. Jesus Christ is my all-sufficient savior. I go to him. God bless & keep & comfort you, precious one, you have been a precious wife to me. To know & love you makes life & death beautiful. Cherish the darlings & give my love to all the dear ones. Do not grieve too much for me. We shall all soon meet. Live for the children. Give my dearest love to Father, mother and Sallie & John. Oh how happy to feel yourself forgiven. God bless you evermore precious, precious one.
>
> Ever yours
> Lawrence[3]

Notice that he expressed no bitterness, no second-guessing, no recrimination toward his commanders. His words were few, but reflected the confidence and contentment that comes with assurance of salvation and a belief in God's divine providence. Incidentally, Chamberlain surprised the physicians and survived his wound, returned home to his wife and family, eventually served four terms as governor of Maine, and lived until age ninety-four. The Sovereign God of Providence had a different plan for him in that field hospital that day. The doctrine of Divine Providence, when properly understood, allows a Christian leader to stabilize in days of defeat and adversity as well as to remain in touch with reality when victorious.

Competency

And finally comes *competency*. The exercise of Christian *character* rooted in sound biblical *content* produces a trustworthy *competency* in a Christian leader. And competent leaders affect everything around them—not as thermometer leaders but as thermostat leaders. How specifically do they do it? Here's how:

A thermostat leader will be used by the Lord to change the lives of God's people by *modeling, mentoring, motivating, managing,* and *ministering.*

A thermostat leader will make an impact on those who look to him by *modeling,* consistently demonstrating growth and maturity with a measure of transparency and permeated by humility. Why the transparency? Because a Christian leader never pretends perfection—only Christ is perfect—but the leader *can and should* model spiritual growth: acknowledging the common struggles of life, readily confessing sin, making the improvements that reflect a heart that is surrendered and growing in grace. The transparency of a Christ-centered life of character yields a powerful model. Followers are taught and strengthened by exposure to a leader who is sensitive to sin, careful in conduct, and humbly committed to honoring the Lord with a faithful witness. Why humility? Because Christian leaders realize that they are what they are only by the grace of God, thus progress in the Christian life is worn with humility and graciousness.

An unforgettable example of such modeling stands for us in the sixteenth-century ministry of William Tyndale, the English clergyman who was put to death during the Reformation for translating the Bible into the English language. Pursued and persecuted—driven from his native England into hiding on the European continent—Tyndale courageously continued his work until the first English New Testament was printed in 1526. When most of the copies were obtained and burned by church officials, Tyndale promptly went back to work and produced another printing. Eventually, however, while working on a translation of the Old Testament, William Tyndale was betrayed, captured, and executed. His last words: "Lord! Open the king of England's eyes."

But as a believer and a translator, Tyndale had faithfully served as a model for one of his assistants—a protégé named Miles Coverdale. Valiantly and skillfully, Coverdale completed Tyndale's translation of the Old Testament and arranged the first printing of the entire Bible in English—the Coverdale Bible—in 1535.

Copies flooded England, and the English people embraced it. Popular demand for the English Bible soon became so strong that King Henry finally bowed to public acclaim and ordered an "Authorized Version." It became known as the "Great Bible," led the way to the most popular English translation in history, the King James Bible, and was providentially printed by the man who had learned from the model of William Tyndale—Miles Coverdale.

Now how should Christian leaders *mentor?* They teach, coach, and instruct. As individuals, they will find various ways to do it, but they will always attempt to help others identify and respond biblically to the issues of life. Effective mentoring also requires committing to be with those who are being mentored, and that requires patience. Patience requires a genuine love for those who are being mentored. Patience also leads to determination and perseverance. And it often requires forgiveness when those who are being coached fail, falter, and at times wonder.

A thermostat leader is also a *motivator.* Motivators know when to speak, what to speak, and how to speak, and they know what to do and what *not* to do in order to inspire their disciples. They avoid crossing the line from uplifting motivation into destructive manipulation. For all believers, the love of Christ, which "controls us" (2 Cor. 5:14), is the primary motivation for every aspect of life. To a lesser degree, but importantly, we are influenced by valid motivational dynamics. As a parent, I quickly learned that all three of my children were different and were motivated by different methods. One child was motivated by competition. If I simply asked, "Do you think you can do this?" it would probably be done. Another child was motivated by the quest for excellence. "Do you think you can beat your old time at running the 3200 meters?" I might ask—and the race was on. The third child was motivated by relationships and affirmation. Doing things together became motivation, and genuine affirmation of each valid achievement became a springboard to the next one.

In the final analysis, a motivator appeals to the great aspirations and ideals of life, while introducing followers to the infallible power that comes through a relationship with Jesus Christ. "Apart from me [Christ] you can do nothing," proclaims John 15:5—and "I can do all things through [Christ] who strengthens me," affirms Philippians 4:13. That's the assurance we have as believers—a mighty motivation—and it's not just success that enables us to honor Christ. It's also the way we handle disappointments and defeats. Thermostat leaders understand that we should strive to live for Christ in all honorable endeavors—even in the messiness of a fallen world in which we encounter good times and bad times. Our desire is to motivate others and influence them to trust the wisdom, grace, and power of their God and Savior to "stay the course" and take life to the next level for the glory of God.

A thermostat leader also strives to be an effective *manager*. Granted, not every leader is a manager—and certainly not every manager is a leader—but those who are called as biblical leaders must be certain that those in their care have the provisional benefits of effective administration and management. Sometimes this is simply a matter of responsible delegation, but it is absolutely essential, and the ultimate responsibility for it lies with the leader. Motivation inspires ardor, but management is necessary for order. Motivation produces passion. Management produces precision. Both are necessary for effective, balanced thermostat leadership.

My maternal grandfather was a memorable example of the management competency. When I was a boy, my Granddaddy could fix anything, but I was puzzled by his habitual method of approaching a challenge. Every time he began a project, he first sat down with a pencil and paper and silently thought and scribbled for what seemed to be *hours*. I finally asked him why we couldn't just *get started*. "We are not ready yet," he told me. "I'm studying on it." Of course, I was impatient, ready to plunge in, but after a while I came to understand what he meant by "studying on it." He planned each job. Before he invested a moment of work on the task, he figured out what needed to be done and what materials were necessary to do it. Had a job been left to me, I would have repeatedly climbed up and down a ladder because of all the things I had forgotten to bring to the task. When my grandfather went up a ladder to do a job, it took one trip. He had everything he needed because he had "studied on it." Management skills are crucial for leadership because they dramatically increase our effectiveness. Effective leaders first learn to manage themselves and then bring thoughtful management and its blessings to the task of leadership. They "study on it." The result is that the job gets done with integrity and insight and those engaged encounter minimal frustrations and distractions.

Finally, thermostat leaders must be *ministers*—therefore they must have a servant's heart. The thirteenth chapter of John reports that Peter protested when Jesus began to wash his disciples' feet in the upper room on the eve of the crucifixion. Jesus listened, addressed Peter's objections, and then finished the task. One by one, he washed the feet of everyone who was present. Then he issued a key command to all his followers for all time, a call to servanthood: "If I then, your Lord and Teacher, have washed your feet," he said, "you also ought to wash one another's feet" (John 13:14).

When I graduated from Westminster Seminary South, which was then called the Florida Theological Center, I remember the sense of accomplishment that I felt when walking across the stage to receive my diploma—and the final lesson imparted to me by the school. The dean of faculty gave me my diploma, shook my hand, and put the Master of Divinity hood over my shoulders. Then he handed me a towel bearing my initials, which hangs in my office today. A towel. "You have now graduated with a theological degree, and you are ready for a call to the pastorate," he said. "This seminary's objective is done. You are equipped and knowledgeably qualified. In fact, you are equipped and qualified for the greatest privilege of all—the gospel ministry. Now, here is your towel. You are qualified to wash the feet of the saints."

The Word of God calls us to be servant leaders. We lead by serving. And that's one of the key differences between a thermostat leader and a thermometer leader. It's not easy to practice servanthood, and it's not easy to be a servant leader. But that's the calling of a biblical leader, and that's the kind of leadership so desperately needed in American culture today. So what's a thermostat leader? The answer: a leader of *character* who applies sound theological *content* in a way that yields a *competent* ministry, one who *models, mentors, motivates, manages, and ministers*—all with the heart of a servant. Challenging? Absolutely. Impossible? Not at all—it's God's way, revealed in God's Word; and what God requires of us, God will enable us to do.

When hearts are surrendered in humble obedience, out of love to Christ and a desire to serve Christ, God can and will make a thermostat leader.

So where do we start?

8

LEARNING, LIVING, LEADING

"Of Issachar [were] men who had understanding of the times,
to know what Israel ought to do. . . ."
1 CHRONICLES 12:32

Past. Present. Future. What do they have in common with great leaders? The answer: great leaders *learn from the past, live in the present,* and *lead to the future.* That's especially true of Bible-based leadership. Lessons from the past are especially meaningful to Christian leaders who follow the biblical model of leadership. History is replete with relevant lessons in leadership—especially military history. In fact, the biblical model of leadership has more in common with combat leadership than with corporate leadership. But, you might respond, combat seems decidedly un-Christian. True—when speaking of this world's combat. But what about otherworldly combat—spiritual warfare? Think about it. God's church is constantly engaged in spiritual warfare. Spiritual warfare is not a subset of the Christian life; it *is* the Christian life. Therefore, Christian leaders are really combat leaders. They know they have an adversary. They know they are under assault. Thankfully, this war has already been won at the cross of Christ. The "whole armor of God" (Eph. 6:11) is sufficient for the soldiers of Christ to stand firm, and the "weapons of the Spirit" are powerfully designed by the Lord to take captive the minds and hearts of men and women. Even so, spiritual warfare—Christian combat—is the rule of the day until the Lord returns. In the army of the Lord there will be casualties, self-inflicted wounds, careless wounds, courageous warriors, martyrs for the Lord, and eventual victory.

Learning from the Past

It is astounding the number of times that God memorialized his good deeds for his people: sometimes by piling up stones, sometimes with a psalm or song, and sometimes with a meal, like the Passover. Why did he do this? His instruction was that they were to bring their children back to that historic moment and teach them what great things their God had done. Then they would learn from the past to impact the present to change the future. "Jesus Christ is the same yesterday and today and forever . . ." (Heb. 13:8).

We are blessed with many classic examples of godly men and women in history. It's often said in Christian circles that history is really *his*-story. We don't want to be preoccupied with the past or live in the past, but there's much to be learned from history—especially from those military leaders who were also serious soldiers of Christ. Consider George Washington. No deist he, contrary to modern humanist propaganda; Washington was a devout believer whose faith sustained him in the darkest days of the American Revolution. At one point in the war—the winter of 1777–1778—the future surely appeared grim to Washington, who was then the commanding general of the Continental Army. The British had driven Washington's army from New York, across New Jersey, and into Pennsylvania. The nation's fledgling capital, Philadelphia, had been captured. The Pennsylvania State House, where the Declaration of Independence had been signed, was occupied by British troops. The Continental Congress had been forced to flee the city, and Washington's army was ragged, hungry, unpaid, and left shivering in winter camp at Valley Forge, Pennsylvania.

American victory was impossible, some believed—including some of the nation's leading clergymen. But Washington was a man of faith, and he would not give up. He was determined to persevere despite the mighty hosts arrayed against him. And he did. He used the bitter months in winter camp to drill his soldiers, inspiring them and encouraging them to believe that they could indeed prevail. Out of his own pocket he resourced chaplains to conduct worship services. When the army emerged from Valley Forge in the spring, it was better than ever—and was prepared to face the worst that the enemy had to offer. Eventually, many of the same soldiers who had limped through the snows of Valley Forge were present to experience what had once seemed unthinkable: the surrender of Lord Cornwallis's British army at Yorktown. Long before that surrender, when victory seemed dim and a defeat loomed, George Washington firmly clung to a belief in the providence of God. "The Hand of providence has been so conspicuous in all this," he wrote in 1778, "that he must be worse than an infidel that lacks faith, and more than wicked, that has not gratitude enough to acknowledge his obligations."[1]

Lesson learned from the past: Christian leaders must equip themselves with the armor of God, take up the weapons of God, and stand firm. We cannot expect followers to go beyond their leaders. Because Christ has defeated Satan and the kingdom of darkness at the cross, we may confidently lead our people forward. And when they are discouraged, by God's grace they will see that their leaders are confident in the Lord for they have learned their lessons well—the battle is not ours but his, and he who has won the victory will do it again in us and through us.

Living in the Present

Great leaders learn from the past, but they refuse to live in the past. Nor are they paralyzed in life waiting for the future. Instead, their focus is on the present and fulfilling their mission and calling. This is crucial, as pointed out in the life of an Old Testament leader, King David, in Acts 13:36: "David, after he had served the purpose of God in his own generation, fell asleep and was laid with his fathers. . . ." The two key phrases in this verse are: "served the purpose of God" and "in his own generation." David had a call and mission from God, and at his best he provided leadership to fulfill God's purpose, thereby allowing him to affect "his own generation." David himself surely knew the history of his people—past lessons of how God had worked over time—and he certainly cared about the future, but his primary focus was to fulfill "God's purpose in his own generation." God has a time and a place for his leaders. To be effective, they must know the Word of God *and* the world around them—the present. Knowing the Word of God equips us to connect through the culture with the transforming power of truth and penetrate the culture while anticipating the impact of God's unstoppable gospel of grace. It will change people and the world in which they live. But, if we wade into the waves of the world without knowing the Word, we can expect a pounding—something I learned as a youthful believer.

I became a Christian while I was a college student. As a "new creation" in Christ (2 Cor. 5:17), I went back to class with a new vigor to learn. I also attempted to proclaim Christ boldly—and sometimes rashly. I was one of about three hundred students enrolled in a psychology class taught by a graduate student who routinely attacked the Bible and the Lord. So I spoke up. The discussions that resulted from my attempt to defend the faith displayed my passion for the Lord, but also revealed my obvious need for discipleship and time in the Word. The Lord at times blessed my attempts to make a good defense despite my shortcomings, but I often took a pounding. I remember standing outside the psychology building after class one day, fielding questions from dozens of fellow students concerning the exchange they had witnessed between the teacher and me. My heart was right, but I needed the maturity and wisdom that comes from investing time in the Word and being discipled by a mature believer. How I would have rejoiced to see Josh McDowell cutting through that crowd and coming to my rescue. Did God produce fruit through me—and often in spite of me? Certainly. He was faithful, but I could have represented him better in those days if I had been well grounded in his Word.

Just as we must study the Word, we must also study the world. Doing so enables a leader to understand the "spirit of the age"— the issues and culture of the day. That's necessary to become a change agent for the Lord. But remember that a Christian leader is to shape the culture; the culture must not shape the leader. Therefore, we must be alert, constantly examining ourselves lest we become like the world as we are attempting to impact the world. It's easy to accommodate the world with the best of motives. It's easy today, for instance, to lose our focus in worship with the best of motives. Contemporary American culture has two obsessions: entertainment and freedom of choice. In an attempt to evangelize (the best of motives), many churches have trumped worship in the name of evangelism thus creating an oxymoron of seeker-centered worship. We *can* do both—worship God in a way that draws seekers to Christ through God-centered worship and seek the lost to bring them to Christ that they might rejoice and give praise and worship to their God and Savior.

But wait—the opposite approach is equally unbiblical. Some churches today are so disinterested in evangelism (resulting in making the Great Commission the "great omission") that they have become distant islands toward which seekers must swim alone in order to be rescued. Furthermore, even if seekers make it to that distant shore, they find themselves in a religious museum dedicated to bygone achievements rather than a movement of God's saving and transforming grace. In response to this, many churches have swung the pendulum and in the name of attracting seekers have installed methods of evangelism that actually become counterproductive to the message of the gospel. Even the best of motives, if attached to unbiblical practices, will produce less than desirable results.

Remember, biblical worship is God-centered, not seeker-centered or believer-centered. Like our culture, today's seekers and many believers are focused on being entertained. Granted, some worship services seem designed to stifle joy or reject reverence, but genuine, biblically defined, God-centered worship will attract seekers and encourage believers. Yet with authentic, God-centered worship, 1 Corinthians 14:25 informs us, the unbeliever will fall on his face "and declare that God is really among you." Note that the verse reveals that God is "really among" us as the center of worship—not believers, not even seekers. "Not to us, O LORD, not to us," says Psalm 115:1, "but to your name give glory for the sake of your steadfast love and your faithfulness!" Lovingly pursuing the lost that they might become seekers of Christ is not accomplished by pandering to the world. But, in the name of a good motive—evangelism—our pandering has reached the depths of abandonment of gospel truth. Instead of truth and love from pastor/leaders, today's sermon titles and topics and many musical lyrics resemble the titles of popular magazines: *Self*, *Us*, *We*, *Me*, and *People*. Much of the contemporary American church in the name of evangelism attempts to make Christianity simply one more self-esteem–boosting therapeutic model with Jesus as the genie in the bottle who offers health, wealth, power, and purpose. God does not exist to give us possessions and purpose. He *is* our purpose and we are his possession. Even more, he is our passion, and his gospel calls us to the glory of dying to self and living for Christ. We must understand the prevailing culture in order to address it, but we must avoid being like the world even as we are in it. Instead, Christian leaders help raise up new leaders who will be like the tribe of Issachar in 1 Chronicles 12:32—those leaders had an "understanding of the times, to know what Israel ought to do."

Changing the Future

Grounded in the Word, aware of the surrounding culture, and tutored from history, effective leaders lead to the future. Some leaders can see the trajectory of the culture into the future and take advantage of it, but what is needed are Christian leaders who are able to change the trajectory of the culture as it moves into the future. Okay, how?

Great Leaders Impart a Biblical Vision. To impart vision a leader must avoid "the paralysis of analysis." Christian leaders must not begin before they know where they are going, and certainly being aware of the world into which their leadership is headed is absolutely essential. But some leaders become incapacitated by indecision. They fail to advance because they fear that they don't have enough information to make a decision, and therefore they are constantly changing their decisions. Effective, biblically based leaders are not indecisive; they have a vision that is biblically defined and culturally connected. With the power of the gospel and the preeminence of Christ in deed and word, they seek to impart it. "Where there is no prophetic vision the people cast off restraint," Scripture advises us in Proverbs 29:18. A future-oriented leader has a vision—imparted by knowing the Word, studying the past, and understanding "his generation." Equipped with the indwelling presence and power of the Spirit of God, a leader is then positioned to impart a vision for the future. Where is God leading the church? The leader's family? The leader's ministry or business? You cannot begin a journey, much less take others with you, unless you know where you are going.

When I step up on the first tee to play a round of golf, I have two swing thoughts—actually two prayer requests: "Lord, please do not let me embarrass myself in front of everyone," and "Lord, please allow me to find this ball after I hit it." When Tiger Woods steps on the first tee, I am sure those prayer requests are not his swing thoughts. In his mind, he is already on the green, putting for a birdie. To be there on the green, there is a certain place in the fairway where he needs to land his tee shot. Now he is ready to hit his drive off the tee. Lesson? *In leadership you begin from the end.* "Lord, why am I here in this leadership position? I am to lead to a destination." That is the vision, and it must be continually imparted to those whom you are taking to that destination.

Great Leaders Are Self-Starters Who Value Humility. By God's grace and the power of the Holy Spirit, effective leaders become self-starters. Christian leaders are nourished by the love of God in Christ and guided by the truth of his Word. This means that they have an innate desire to do their best at all times. The result is they are constantly seeking genuine spiritual growth in life and ministry to honor the Lord. They live out or "work out [their] own salvation with fear and trembling," according to Philippians 2:12. With humility and a servant's heart, they seek to grow spiritually as well as develop their effectiveness as servant leaders. That is why biblical leaders are not threatened when their ministry or organization establishes performance evaluations, but instead welcome the opportunity for accountability and improvement. They are aware of God's numerous scriptural admonitions that he tears down the prideful and exalts the humble. Some leaders exalt themselves and then pray for humility, but the Scripture tells us to do the opposite: "Humble yourselves before the Lord, and he will exalt you" (James 4:10).

One of my most treasured mentors is a powerful preacher, yet even he recounts his "encouragement" to humility. One Sunday, as he drove home from church with his wife, he thought about the sermon he had preached that day. It was perhaps the best sermon he had ever delivered, he told himself. Turning to his wife, a loving and supportive spouse—and an honest, perceptive woman—he posed a question that begged for a U-turn back to a state of humility. Cheerfully, his wife assisted him. "Honey," he asked her, "how many great preachers do you think there are in the United States? I mean, how many *really* great preachers?" His wife looked at him for a moment, then blandly replied: "Honey, I don't know how many there are. But I do know this: there is one less than you think."

Great Leaders Establish a Means of Personal Accountability. Great leaders find a way to make sure that they are accountable to others. Perhaps it's an accountability partner. Or a group. Or the church elders. They meet regularly for prayer, sharing, caring, and self-improvement before the Lord. It's also wise for a leader to have a formal evaluation team composed of insightful elders or other church leaders. The team should meet regularly to evaluate and offer encouragement, observation, and instruction. It's good for the leader, it's good for the group, and, if effective, it will be good for the church or organization.

Great Leaders Focus on the Fundamentals. In his autobiography, *My Story*, the great professional golfer Jack Nicklaus revealed the benefits of a focused and disciplined life. Every year throughout his spectacular career, Nicklaus went back home to Ohio to spend time with a local golf pro named Jack Grout, who was Nicklaus's longtime mentor and golf teacher. Together they would go to the practice tee, where Nicklaus always began the new season with the same request: "Jack Grout, teach me how to play golf." Grout would respond by going through the basics of the game as if the great Nicklaus were an untrained amateur. They would play the course that way, with Nicklaus again in the role of the student, learning the fundamentals of the game from his teacher. Jack Nicklaus knew that the key to playing great golf lay in focusing on the basics. Leadership is the same: greatness and effectiveness come from continually refining and building upon the basics with a commitment to excellence. Derek Jeter, arguably the best shortstop in the major leagues, will go to spring training every year and take hundreds of ground balls and hundreds of swings in the batting cage preparing for the next year. Greatness seldom is a matter of exotic ingenuity but usually flows from the ability of a leader to stay focused on the basics and execute them with excellence.

Great Leaders Are Disciplined. Discipline doesn't come easy to us saved sinners, especially in a sinful world. For most of us, it's a lifelong struggle. But it's a battle worth fighting. Why? Because discipline is a key factor in life and leadership. Growing in the Lord through his Word requires discipline. So does a regular prayer life. And family life. And church. And work. And ministry. And most of whatever else is worthwhile and important in our lives. Leaders who follow the biblical model of leadership grow to become disciplined and intentionally seek to remain so. A disciplined life is not an attempt to earn God's love. Our God has given that love freely in Christ. "We love because he first loved us" (1 John 4:19). A disciplined life is one way that we show our love to God, one way that we worship him by seeking to be consistently faithful, effective, and teachable.

Great leaders—God-centered leaders—refuse to squander their lives to the whims of culture, the fads of the day, the ways of the world. They learn from the past without living in the past. They live in the present without accommodating the present, and they lead to the future without waiting for it. To do so, they learn God's Word, understand the surrounding culture, and seek to impart a biblical mission and vision as grace-filled self-starters—who seek to be accountable, focus on the basics, and live a disciplined lifestyle. In short, they seek to live according to the familiar advice of Proverbs 3:5: "Trust in the LORD with all your heart, and do not lean on your own understanding. In all your ways acknowledge him, and he will make straight your paths." That's not simply a pleasant homily. It's a proverbial promise of wisdom from the God of the ages.

Believe his Word. And when you do, get ready for some amazing experiences as you grow in the Lord and for the Lord. That growth, while potentially dynamic in nature, will focus on four areas. Having *defined* leaders and leadership, just how do you *develop* them?

9

DEVELOPING LEADERS—GOD'S WAY

"And Jesus increased in wisdom and in stature
and in favor with God and man."

LUKE 2:52

A re leaders born or made? Is it by nature or nurture?
The answer is "Yes!" It's both. Some families seem to have
an undiscovered genetic strain that produces generations of
leaders. Other leaders rise from a leaderless heritage. So leaders
are obviously affected by family history and environment, but
it's also obvious that leadership can be learned. For instance, not
every man claims to be a gifted leader, yet the Bible clearly teaches
that every husband and father is supposed to spiritually "lead" his
family. Every believer—man and woman alike—is called to "lead"
others to Christ. So it's obvious that God realizes leadership can
be learned and developed. Those called to leadership who are
not natural leaders can still seek to be faithful and effective by
the nurture of leadership skills. So, however God equips those
called to leadership, they should humbly and purposely seek to
develop their leadership skills.

The New Testament books of 1 and 2 Timothy—Paul's epistles to his protégé Timothy—were inspired by the Holy Spirit and penned by Paul to give Timothy the leadership instruction necessary to carry on Paul's ministry after his death. The book of 1 Timothy also contains the basics of a revitalization ministry that Timothy was to implement at Ephesus: Christ-centered and gospel-driven preaching and teaching, prayer, leadership, evangelism, confessional unity, and worship. Paul's final epistle was 2 Timothy, which he may have written hours before he was executed outside Rome. Just as Elijah passed the mantle of leadership to Elisha in the Old Testament, Paul did the same to Timothy with the pastoral epistle of 2 Timothy. With his last words, Paul presented the biblical model of Three-*D* leadership: he had *defined* leadership for Timothy, he had *developed* Timothy as a leader, and with his final letter he prepared Timothy to be *deployed* as a leader.

As he did so, he exhorted Timothy to develop his leadership skills: "to fan into flame the gift of God, which is in you through the laying on of . . . hands" (2 Tim. 1:6). He also urged Timothy to study the Word of God as "a worker" (2:15), and to "keep a close watch on yourself and on the teaching. Persist in this, for by so doing you will save both yourself and your hearers" (1 Tim. 4:16). The mandate is unmistakable. Leaders must always seek to develop themselves by God's grace, and that requires personal discipline—the discipline of grace. Notice: not discipline *for* grace but the discipline *of* grace. How? By living a lifestyle in which you daily "put off your old self" and "put on the new self" (Eph. 4:22–24). Alone, this task is impossible. But you don't have to do it alone. God provides the means of grace in which his Spirit and his Word will work in your life for your good and his glory and will give you the ability to employ them. Remember this is not self-discipline for grace; it's God's grace that disciplines us.

There is one case of perfect personal development, and obviously that is Jesus. And there is one verse that describes his personal formation: "And Jesus increased in wisdom and in stature and in favor with God and man" (Luke 2:52). Have you ever thought about the model set for us in this familiar verse? Christ is our Redeemer and ultimate example, and here he gives us a simple, profound foundation for personal formation. How did our Lord, in his humanity, grow and develop? The biblical answer: *in wisdom* (intellectual formation), *in stature* (physical formation), *in favor with God* (spiritual formation), and *in favor with man* (relational formation). The Word of God has thus given us a biblically defined plan for personal formation that is far wiser than anything that human ingenuity could produce, and our Savior has given us the power by his transforming grace to enact it.

Wisdom—Intellectual Formation

Wisdom is revealed in the lifestyle of a leader who makes decisions that honor the Lord. Proverbs 9:10 reveals that "the fear of the LORD is the beginning of wisdom." What does that mean—really? It means that we must know who God is and our relationship before him as well as our calling by him. The God who loves us is truly awesome, and we are directed to love him with both intimacy and reverence. His majesty and holiness make it all the more extraordinary that he loves us enough even to mount the cross for us so that we might know him and be with him. So wisdom begins with our understanding of who God is and who we are.

Scripture also teaches that biblical wisdom is ultimately demonstrated in our behavior. "By his good conduct," declares James 3:13, "let him show his works in the meekness of wisdom"; and according to James 3:17, "wisdom from above is first pure, then peaceable, gentle, open to reason, full of mercy and good fruits, impartial and sincere." James is clearly commenting on the three key themes from the book of Proverbs that we should seek: knowledge, understanding, and wisdom. It is not enough to simply have knowledge. Knowledge must be embraced with understanding. True knowledge and understanding will lead to wisdom, which is manifested in a transformed life as James describes. Nowhere in Scripture does God tell us to be "smart." That highly promoted human commodity is obviously not very important to the Creator of the universe. Instead, God wants us to have wisdom—his wisdom—which begins with acknowledging that our loving Father is the God of the ages and living in a manner that honors him and then seeking to obey his Word in all areas of our life. We do that by knowing his Word and applying it thoughtfully to our lives. This is the infallible evidence of a new heart, which is also to be a surrendered heart.

Stature—Physical Formation

The human body is "a temple of the Holy Spirit," proclaims 1 Corinthians 6:19, and the Word commands each of us to "present your bodies as a living sacrifice" (Rom. 12:1). Having a surrendered heart calls us to pursue obedience to these scriptural directives: God's people should strive to live with a regimen of rest, exercise, and diet that honors God. This passage drives that point home: "So, whether you eat or drink, or whatever you do, do all to the glory of God" (1 Cor. 10:31). Christians out of love to Christ should not live to eat, which is idolatry, but instead should eat to live for Christ, which is worship.

We should also be obedient and responsible in obtaining daily rest, and we should observe the Sabbath commandment to worship and rest weekly: "Six days you shall labor, and do all your work, but the seventh day is a Sabbath to the LORD your God" (Ex. 20:9–10). The Lord's Day is God's gift to man, according to Jesus: "The Sabbath was made for man, not man for the Sabbath" (Mark 2:27). When Jesus took the disciples away to pray, they continually fell asleep. His response and analysis were both insightful and pastoral: "the spirit indeed is willing, but the flesh is weak" (Matt. 26:41). In other words, Jesus knew that in their hearts and souls they desired to pray with him but physically they were neither ready nor used to periods of extended prayer.

Paul says that he would buffet his body and make it his slave (1 Cor. 9:27). Why? Paul knew that his ministry was demanding and the challenges daunting. He wanted his body ready for the challenges ahead. The success of physical discipline usually depends upon the vitality of spiritual discipline; spiritual discipline impacts physical discipline. The fruit of the Spirit passage concludes by affirming the promised blessing of "self-control" (Gal. 5:22). Then, the physical disciplines position us to focus upon the priorities of spiritual growth. If we stay up late on Saturday night, normally we will not be able to worship the Lord with spiritual vitality on Sunday morning. As one preacher has said, "*Saturday Night Live* will be Sunday morning dead." Your body is not a container that carries your spirit and soul. Your body is like a single thread, and your spirit and soul is another thread. These two threads are woven into one cloth, which is your life. What you do to one inevitably will affect the other. Grace-enabled spiritual growth will inevitably encourage physical discipline, and physical discipline positions you for greater spiritual growth. So let's examine the disciplines of spiritual formation.

Favor with God—Spiritual Formation

A healthy spiritual life is the result of Christ-centered disciple making. Why don't true followers of Christ embrace the lifestyle of a Christ-centered disciple and disciple maker? Here are some reasons.

An Inability to Say "No." As Christians, we're called to seek a simple life. 1 Thessalonians 4:11 advises us to "aspire to live quietly, and to mind your own affairs." Simplicity in life requires being willing and able to say "no." Most Christians are too busy. We have allowed the world to set our life's schedule, resulting in ineffective busyness. We have lost the ability to prioritize in general. And we have lost an understanding of biblical priorities in particular. In Luke 10, our Lord was enjoying the hospitality of two sisters, Martha and Mary. Mary was sitting "at the Lord's feet" listening to his teaching. In contrast, Martha "was distracted with much serving." She then, sharply, inquires of the Lord, "Do you not care that my sister has left me to serve alone? Tell her then to help me." The Lord's answer was instructive and challenging. "Martha, Martha. You are anxious and troubled about many things but one thing is necessary. Mary has chosen the good portion which will not be taken away from her" (Luke 10:38–42). There was obviously nothing wrong with Martha's commitment to serve. What our Lord was affirming was Mary's commitment to making the right priority decision. Effective serving in life is assured by prioritizing time with the Lord in his Word. Mary had made a good choice of a right priority. Out of that she would be able to serve, but serving should not trump one's commitment to prioritizing the hearing of God's Word. Mary had made the right "choice" and therefore had created an appropriate priority in life.

You can't say "no" until you have a bigger "yes." To have a bigger "yes," you have to know God's priorities from his Word, which also gives you the biblical principles to make wise decisions. Establishing and maintaining biblical priorities and properly ordering our lives is not easy for Christian leaders. We love people and we want to serve people, plus there is an ever-subtle desire to be busy because we think that busyness tells other people that we are important. Find God's "yeses" from his Word. A biblical "yes" will be big enough for you to say "no" appropriately and kindly but firmly and at the right time.

Shortchanging Your Alone Time with the Lord. Examine the lifestyle of a ministry leader who has failed, and you'll frequently find a lack of personal time with the Lord. Often, even among mature ministers, the first thing sacrificed to an overly demanding lifestyle is their time alone with God. If you are not exercising a daily relationship with the Lord, you're much more likely to stumble or fall. You need times of silence, reflection, and renewal. Psalm 62:1 says it perfectly: "For God alone my soul waits in silence. . . ."

Living Beyond Your Means. Advertising agencies are committed to making yesterday's luxuries today's necessities, and they are extremely effective in their marketing schemes. Too many Christians in today's materialistic world, including Christian leaders, find themselves with "too much month at the end of the money" because they have bought into a conspicuous consumer lifestyle. How do you avoid that materialistic trap in today's consumer-driven culture? Here's a simple plan: First say "no" to idolatry, then write down the income that God has given you. Subtract the tithe and the offerings that you feel led to give beyond the tithe. Then arrange a lifestyle that works with what's left. Adopt a lifestyle within your means, and don't automatically expand it when your income increases. While debt is not sin, you can be sinfully in debt. Conspicuous consumerism is driven by having to get the next thing with a conspicuous label, believing that this is the key to a meaningful life. Actually that is idolatry. Our Lord will give us what we need, and if he gives us more, it may be for the purpose of expanding our ministry. How much you have does not immediately concern me. What does concerns me is, does what you have actually have you? Matthew 6:33 tells us to "seek first the kingdom of God and his righteousness, and all these things will be added to you." Too many of us seek things and let the Lord be added unto us. Life is not in things; "to live is Christ." Things are not our life. "For what does it profit a man to gain the whole world and forfeit his soul?" (Mark 8:36). Don't let things use you and draw you away from him who loves you and has loosed you from your sins (Rev. 1:5).

Forfeiting the Opportunity to Give Sacrificially. What a blessing it is to give sacrificially of our time, energy, or money. When we learn to live within our means and spend our time wisely by living with simplicity, we establish margins from which we are then able to respond to opportunities of ministry and giving sacrificially. Don't forfeit those God-given opportunities with a careless or materialistic lifestyle. If you live within your means—willing to say "no" when it's appropriate and managing finances responsibly—you can give sacrificially when God presents a need. Living a disciplined lifestyle, one that is surrendered to the Lord and based on his Word, will allow you to have the ability to give of your time, energy, and money because your simplicity will have created margins in your life. Do it, and you'll be repeatedly reminded that it really is "more blessed to give than to receive" (Acts 20:35).

Neglecting to Fast—With Prayer and the Word. Reluctant to fast? Do you associate it with hunger strikes and grim-faced self-denial? Or with boastful adherents who proudly (and unbiblically) announce that they're fasting? Well, forget those notions. They're parodies of genuine fasting, which is a blessing that comes in various forms. It's not self-inflicted punishment; it's devotion—and you shouldn't neglect it. It's simply a joyful exercise of setting aside a habitual act in exchange for a calculated focus on the Lord. Fasting should always be accompanied by prayer and the Word. Skip lunch once in a while and spend that time in the Word and prayer. Set aside your hobby occasionally and give that time to the Lord. Devote a break time to Scripture instead of Starbucks. Set aside a day and spend it in devotional Bible reading, prayer, meditation, and time to be alone with God. What a joy. What a feast. What a blessing. Keep it to yourself—the biblical admonition in Matthew 6:16–18 is to tell nobody but the Lord that you're fasting. Then enjoy the blessings that result from a special moment of intimacy with the God who loves you.

Succumbing to Sexual Sin. It's so obviously wrong—yet it's so incredibly common. Outright adultery is painfully plentiful in ministry leadership, and pornography is even more pervasive. Don't succumb to it! Remember the biblical fall of King David, which began with idleness, roving eyes, and a lustful response, then descended to adultery and murder. Stop the downfall when it's a spark, not a flame—and certainly before it's a wildfire. Don't trust yourself? Good—you shouldn't. Flee temptation and fill your heart with a love for Christ and a love for your spouse. When a heart is filled there is no room for the obsessions of sexual idolatry. Ask the Lord to give you a revulsion to even think of sexual immorality and an obsession with the joy of the marriage bed, which is holy. Then, find those of the same gender who will love you enough to pray for you and hold you accountable while encouraging you to "fix your eyes on Jesus." Remember that a saved sinner is still a sinner, and never put yourself in harm's way. Never. And never rely on your own strength: "Put no confidence in the flesh" (Phil. 3:3).

Now, we are ready to grow. The new life is vibrant and vital, but it must always be regularly and abundantly nourished. Historically we have called these biblically ordained practices of personal spiritual nourishment the "means of grace." They enable you to strengthen and deepen the intimacy of your relationship with the Lord. Let's examine them.

Personal Prayer Life. In Matthew 6:6, the Lord instructs us to find a time and a place where we can privately come to him in prayer. We endanger our spiritual health when we neglect having a quiet time, but we receive great blessings when we make it a priority. The demands on leaders may be greater, but the need for a consistent quiet time is also greater. You need regular time alone with God. All children need some alone time with their father, and you do, too—with your heavenly Father.

Personal Bible Study. Prayer and the Word should be inseparable. Christian leaders need systematic, focused time in the Word of God. It's that simple. And that vital. Perhaps this practice that has helped me will help you: Have a sacred place and a sacred time that you meet the Lord to be nourished in him through his Word and prayer each day. Mine is in the morning, so before I go to bed, I go to the appointed place where I will meet the Lord at the appointed time the next morning and place my Bible, my journal, and my devotional material there. Haven't you noticed that when someone sets the table, we always seem to make it to the table to be fed and nourished? So, set the spiritual table the night before. It will assist you in the discipline of arriving there with expectation the next day.

Memorization and Meditation. Having encountered God's Word through personal Bible study and drawn close to the Lord in personal prayer, every believer has the opportunity to enhance this moment through memorization of and meditation on the Word of God. Sadly, contemporary American culture is so adrift that many people equate meditation with Eastern mysticism. How far we have strayed! Transcendental meditation—grievously popular even in our churches today—is the emptying of the mind for the purpose of self-absorption. In contrast, meditation on the Word of God is the intentional filling of heart and mind with God's revealed truth, which is illuminated by his Holy Spirit.

Meditation on his Word inspires us, comforts us, directs us, and protects us from sin, as noted in Psalm 119:11: "I have stored up your word in my heart, that I might not sin against you." Memorization enables us to always be prepared to meditate on God's Word, and meditation leads us to reflection—applying the Word to our personal situation. It's a glorious and essential exercise in a believer's personal relationship with Jesus Christ and will usually lead to the realization of our sins and that we have "fallen short of the glory of God" (Rom. 3:23). That leads us to our next discipline.

Confession. Through reflection, the Holy Spirit convicts us of our sins. Remember, Satan wants to condemn us, to make us feel worthless, and to pull us down and away from God. That's condemnation, which Satan wants to use to discourage us as God's ambassadors. In contrast, true Holy Spirit conviction prompts us to confess our sins and repent with full assurance that God will forgive us and "renew a right spirit within [us]" (Ps. 51:10). That's God's way of drawing us back to him in order to know his love. Satan condemns and neutralizes; God convicts and inspires. So keep "short accounts" with God by being ever ready to confess sin when he convicts you. Remember, "If we confess our sins," we're promised in 1 John 1:9, "he is faithful and just to forgive us our sins and to cleanse us from all unrighteousness."

Consecration. Forgiveness is granted to believers once and for all time through God's grace by the finished work of Jesus Christ on the cross. As we exercise our relationship with him in prayer, through the Word, meditating, reflecting, and confessing sin, we experience the ongoing joy of our salvation. And by God's grace we are refreshed, renewed, and empowered to consecrate ourselves to his service. To *consecrate* means to "set apart or dedicate," and Bible-based leadership should be exercising every means of grace to do that in an ever-growing lifestyle of intimacy with the Lord. The lyrics of the old hymn "Just as I Am, Thine Own to Be" have it right: "To consecrate myself to Thee, O Jesus Christ, I come. . . ."

Favor with Man—Relational Development

As we confront the culture, believers in general and *Christian leaders* in particular must do so with the love of Christ. The model that the Lord gives us in Luke 2:52 calls us to increase in *favor with man*, which means the people of this world, both lost and saved. Those who are not believers should see Jesus in us. We should be different, and one difference should be a loving, caring heart. Our relationships with nonbelievers should be genuine, loving, and respectful. That will open the door for effective evangelism. Other believers should see Christ in us, too, and be encouraged by that same loving, Christ-filled heart. Exhibiting the love of Christ should be the goal of every believer—and it is absolutely essential to effective Christian leadership.

Do you want to model Christ as a leader? Embrace the love of Christ: sacrificial, humble, selfless love. Again, you cannot do it alone—nobody can—but by God's grace and empowered by his Holy Spirit, you can indeed radiate the love of Christ. What a witness it is to the lost, and what an encouragement it is to the saved.

An old adage (which my wife has framed in needlepoint in our home) makes a powerful point: "The greatest thing a father can do for his children is to love their mother." How true it is, and how influential is the love of a husband toward a wife. Even more powerful and influential is the love of Christ shown to others through us. This ought to be like needlepoint on the heart of every Christian leader: "The greatest thing a child of God can do for his Father is to show the Father's love to others."

As a leader, you must remember that all our relationships with others are affected by our relationship with the Lord. If you want to be a leader who models Christ, who increases in favor with man, you must be serious about increasing your knowledge of the favor of God provided for you in Christ, your Lord and Savior. Our intimate relationship with him must increasingly be genuine, vibrant, and vigorous. The result of being intimate with Christ will be demonstrated by the love of Christ permeating our human relationships. In John 13:35, all believers—leaders included—are at once both admonished and encouraged by the Lord: "By this all people will know that you are my disciples, if you have love for one another."

Before going as a leader, we must be growing in our Lord. So grow.

In wisdom.

In stature.

In favor with God.

And in favor with man.

Now you are prepared to lead for the Lord. But now, what do you do to be used of the Lord so that others are enabled to grow and go with you?

10

RANCHER OR SHEPHERD: WHICH ARE YOU?

"I am the good shepherd.
The good shepherd lays down his life for the sheep."

JOHN 10:11

Are you a rancher or a shepherd?

What's the difference, you might ask, and why does it matter? Good questions. It matters a lot if you're a Christian leader. Ranchers drive herds and shepherds lead flocks. It's that simple. Ranchers crack the whip and create fear. Shepherds call the sheep by name and set the pace.

I once saw this firsthand in Israel. In the countryside outside Jerusalem, I noticed a flock of sheep in the distance. As I watched the flock's Bedouin shepherd, I realized that he was not driving the flock from behind, but was leading it from the front. His rod and staff were not used for driving the sheep, but were available for tending and defending them. I could hear him singing and occasionally calling those who were wandering away. The sheep knew his voice, and he knew his sheep—he called them by name—and they calmly followed him. It's no accident that the Lord refers to his beloved, the redeemed, as sheep and not cattle, nor is it accidental that he delights in picturing his leadership as a Good Shepherd. Go to the high country of Wyoming today and you'll sometimes see a white dot on a faraway mountain meadow. It's a sheep wagon—the shepherd's home. The shepherd will stay with his flock in the remote upland meadows for the entire summer, isolated by choice from the rest of the world. Why? Simply to take care of the sheep. Being a shepherd requires a sacrificial lifestyle. The Lord knew that when he gave us the analogy of his people as sheep and his leaders as shepherds in John 10:1–11:

> Truly, truly, I say to you, he who does not enter the sheepfold by the door but climbs in by another way, that man is a thief and a robber. But he who enters by the door is the shepherd of the sheep. To him the gatekeeper opens. The sheep hear his voice, and he calls his own sheep by name and leads them out. When he has brought out all his own, he goes before them, and the sheep follow him, for they know his voice. A stranger they will not follow, but they will flee from him, for they do not know the voice of strangers.

Jesus used this allegory, "but they did not understand what he was saying to them. So Jesus again said to them, 'Truly, truly, I say to you, I am the door of the sheep. All who came before me are thieves and robbers, but the sheep did not listen to them. I am the door. If anyone enters by me, he will be saved and will go in and out and find pasture. The thief comes only to steal and kill and destroy. I came that they may have life and have it abundantly. I am the good shepherd. The good shepherd lays down his life for the sheep.'" (John 10:6–11)

A Christian Leader Is a Shepherd

What an extraordinary model. Look at it carefully. First, a shepherd knows his sheep, and they "know his voice." Obviously, the Lord does this to perfection with every believer in ways beyond our abilities as sinful, though saved, leaders. Think, however, about how Christian leaders can apply this model in leading their flocks. Knowing your sheep so well that they know your voice requires an investment of *love, time,* and *attention*: a love for the Lord and your people that motivates you to exercise your call; the time necessary to know the needs of your people and to be there for them; and the attention necessary to respond to their needs and to do so promptly and consistently. Do you have so many sheep in your flock that it's impossible for you to do this personally? Then it's your responsibility to reproduce and develop new shepherd leaders who extend Christ's leadership to his people, so that everyone may be cared for by shepherd leaders. To do so, you will have to lead your leaders in learning the heart and life of a shepherd. Sacrificial and shepherd leadership does not come naturally. It has to be learned. Following the biblical model of leadership means developing healthy leaders who have healthy relationships with those whom they lead. Furthermore, it requires shepherds who care enough to lay down their lives to protect the sheep while seeking more and more to know the sheep and their deepest needs.

Second, while a false shepherd will abandon his sheep in hard times, a true shepherd will lay down his life for his sheep at all times. Again, Christ is our model, and Christ-centered leadership stands in contrast to self-centered leadership. The world's leadership models are self-centered and manipulative, which leads to using and sometimes abusing followers. Worldly leadership is all about power, control, and personal promotion. It's a cattle drive. Sometimes it's effective in reaching a goal, but inevitably it's all about the leader, and those who pay the cost are the followers. Whether it succeeds or fails, it usually leaves behind unbelievable human wreckage. The biblical model of leadership must be distinctively different. It's Christ-centered, not self-centered. The Christian leader who practices Christ-centered leadership shepherds his sheep, which is achieved by positioning himself in front of his flock to lead and set the pace for it. The dramatic contrast between the false shepherd and the good shepherd is that the shepherd pays the cost for the sheep while the false shepherd seeks to profit from the sheep, and therefore the sheep pay the price. In the midst of a terrible tragedy, I saw both examples clearly displayed.

On August 24, 1992, Hurricane Andrew slammed into southern Florida. It was a Category 5 storm, and it hit with the power of an atomic blast. It killed forty people, left a quarter-million people homeless, damaged or destroyed more than eighty thousand businesses, and caused more than $30 billion in damages. I was with a team of believers who traveled to the area to help in the wake of the storm. Homestead, Florida City, and South Miami looked like war zones. We connected with a number of churches in the area. At one of the churches the congregational leadership had established a command center, and the pastor was in charge of directing the response. The church secured status reports on families in the neighborhood—nonmembers as well as members—and a leadership team prioritized the needs. Another team gathered and organized available resources. A smaller team matched the resources with the needs, and then other teams were dispatched to help, providing prayer, food, water, shelter, and other necessities, along with personal encouragement. They did great work at a great cost to themselves. The pastor who directed the operation, as well as the other leaders involved, had all suffered personal losses of some kind, yet they put aside their own needs and sacrificially provided the desperately needed leadership in a Christ-centered manner. They did great work. They served the Lord, their congregation, and their community. It was a powerful witness—shepherding at its best. God's people were cared for, the community was ministered to, and the world saw the witness when a special was aired on ABC television about the church, the leadership, and the ministry. It all began with sacrificial leadership.

Unfortunately, another pastor's response provided a dramatic contrast. We showed up at his church to help, but no one was there. So we made our way to the pastor's home. No one was there, either. Some from the area had been evacuated before the hurricane, but many residents were now returning—including his members—but he was not. He chose to remain evacuated. Certainly he needed to make sure that his family was in a place of safety and was receiving care. But what about his flock? He chose not to return when needed. He failed to be there when his flock needed him the most, and when he could have provided leadership to help and inspire his surrounding neighborhood. It was the opposite of sacrificial, Christ-centered shepherding. His flock, leaderless, was left to depend solely on themselves and others. Thankfully the good providence of God led us there. But what a missed opportunity to serve and manifest the Chief Shepherd's love for his people and establish a caring relationship, which would have allowed him as a leader to build upon in the future! The shepherd of the flock had taken care of himself and avoided much of the pain that most of his people experienced. He also missed the opportunity to be Christ's instrument in the care of his flock. What a missed moment of leadership ministry.

Think about the familiar and instructive words of the Twenty-third Psalm. How reassuring they are. Note the model established for Christian leaders:

> The LORD is my shepherd; I shall not want.
>   He makes me lie down in green pastures.
> He leads me beside still waters.
>   He restores my soul.
> He leads me in paths of righteousness
>   for his name's sake.
> Even though I walk through the valley of the shadow
>   of death,
>   I will fear no evil,
> for you are with me;
>   your rod and your staff,
>   they comfort me.
>
> You prepare a table before me
>   in the presence of my enemies;
> you anoint my head with oil;
>   my cup overflows.

119

Surely goodness and mercy shall follow me
  all the days of my life,
and I shall dwell in the house of the LORD
  forever.

Remember that a shepherd's rod and staff are not for beating the sheep, but for protecting and rescuing them. The blunt end of the staff is used to drive away predators, and the hook on the other end—the crook of the rod—is used to pull them from danger. That's why the passage notes that the rod and staff are a comfort. The passage also establishes the shepherd's commitment to feed the sheep and nourish them in "green pastures" and to rest them beside "still waters." The shepherd, in tending to the needs of the sheep, focuses on the priority work of a shepherd, which is restoring the soul. The sheep have been rescued from potential harm and are assured of everlasting victory through Christ. That's why the familiar "valley" verse describes death as a "shadow," something that is temporary and passing for the believer. Death is only a shadow of what it was before it was overcome by the Great Shepherd in victory. In following this model, shepherd leaders will intentionally commit to addressing the needs of their people ("surely goodness and mercy shall follow me all the days of my life"), particularly their spiritual needs ("I shall dwell in the house of the LORD forever").

A Christian Leader Is a Servant

The Christian leader is also a servant. That's a familiar observation, but sadly, it's one that's often taught and seldom obeyed. Many Christians claim to be servants with a smile—until they're actually treated like one. A ministry leader in Latin America authored a book on servant leadership that sold more than a million copies in the Third World. While it was embraced there, it received very little demand in the United States. Why, asked a publisher, was this fundamental leadership teaching so popular in the Third World, but so ignored in America? It was his conclusion, the author sadly replied, that American ministry leaders want to rule rather than serve. They desire more to be "lords of all" rather than "servants of all."

If that's true, then we are surely leading by the values of the world and not the precepts of the Word. Scripture is clear: Jesus Christ calls us to be leaders who serve, not lords who abuse. Consider the servanthood shown to us in John 13. Scripture reveals that Jesus administered the last old-covenant meal of renewal—the Passover—and then as the living, eternal Passover Lamb, he instituted the new-covenant meal of renewal—the Lord's Supper. In doing so, he fulfilled prophecy: Jesus Christ, God in human form, would take the punishment that we deserve for our sins as the unblemished Lamb of the Passover. And by his atoning sacrifice all who believe in him will be saved. He also left us with an unmistakable model of Christian servant leadership when:

> He laid aside his outer garments, and taking a towel, tied it around his waist. Then he poured water into a basin and began to wash the disciples' feet and to wipe them with the towel that was wrapped around him. (John 13:4–5)

There it is for all of us to see and emulate. Jesus Christ, the Lord God of the ages, did what a household servant was supposed to have done. He took a basin of water and washed the filthy feet of a dozen sandal-wearing men. It was not too lowly for him, and it was not by accident. He did it to deliver an unforgettable lesson to his disciples—and to us. Christian leadership is not lording it over anyone; it's being willing to serve everyone.

Servant leadership does not require much instruction (beyond the exhortation to be servants), but it does require motivation and humility. Instead of striving to be served, Christian leaders strive to serve. And what a dramatic impression servant leadership would make in our self-serving culture, even in little ways. I once played a round of golf with the prominent CEO of a major multinational bank. I had been told that he was a committed believer, and I soon became a beneficiary of and witness to his Christianity and servant leadership. He was a pleasant, friendly fellow, but it wasn't his edifying words that impressed me—it was his seemingly small gestures. On every hole, this influential, wealthy, and acclaimed executive had not only repaired his ball mark on the green according to golf etiquette, but also had repaired everyone else's before we arrived. Not only that, he routinely marked and cleaned everyone's golf ball before he gave it back to them. It was a small act that revealed a large servant's heart. Therefore it was no surprise when I later found out that this Christian leader had created a program that enabled those who were among the working poor to purchase a home at a reasonable price with an appropriate loan structure, as well as carefully thought-out leadership initiatives to elevate his employees and his customers.

A Christian Leader Is a Superintendent

Some Christian leaders have the commitment to be a shepherd and the heart to be a servant, but they're ineffective because they don't secure the blessing of also providing superintendent leadership. They just aren't willing to do the necessary planning for life-changing leadership effectiveness. But that's also a part of God's call to leaders: to be overseers who superintend people, policies, and processes for the benefit of his people. Scripture makes it clear in 1 Timothy 3:4–5 that a leader is a superintendent, beginning with excellence in family management, which positions him for effective church management: "He must manage his own household well, with all dignity keeping his children submissive, for if someone does not know how to manage his own household, how will he care for God's church?"

How do you as a leader learn to be a superintendent in home and church? The answer: by knowing what God expects you to provide for others as revealed in his Word. If you're a husband, for instance, you're commanded to love your wife "as Christ loved the church" (Eph. 5:25). This means that you reflect Christ as Prophet, Priest, and King. As prophet of the home, you're expected to provide spiritual leadership, to be above reproach, to personally see to the spiritual development of your family, and to conduct yourself in a Christ-like manner in thought, word, and deed. Husbands are to lay down their lives for their wives as Christ loved his Bride, to wash her with the water of the Word (Eph. 5:26). As "priest," you're to provide for your family's needs even at the expense of your own with the selfless heart of a servant. As "king," you have the responsibility to lovingly guide your wife and children, to show them respect, and to exercise responsible, caring, and protective leadership.

What about in the church? The same is true: leaders must know from God's Word what he expects them to provide as they superintend the flock of God. If you're in congregational leadership, for instance, you're responsible for oversight of the public "means of grace." When you exercise superintendent leadership, whether in the home or in the church, not only do those in your care grow in the Lord, but so do you. What are the public means of grace and how are they provided to God's people with integrity and consistent effectiveness?

The preaching of the Word. According to Romans 10:17, "faith comes from hearing, and hearing through the word of Christ." The priority of exposing God's Word through preaching to the assembly of his people is a recurring theme throughout Scripture. "God was well-pleased through the foolishness of the message preached to save those who believe" (1 Cor. 1:21, NASB).

Public prayer. Publicly calling on the Lord in prayer is recorded throughout Scripture and is declared necessary and holy. Remember, when Jesus condemned the Pharisees in Matthew 6, he did not condemn public prayer but private prayer being done publicly in order to be seen by others. As for public prayer, Scripture encourages it: "I desire then that in every place the men should pray," proclaims 1 Timothy 2:8, "lifting holy hands. . . ."

Ministry. When a believer with a servant's heart assumes ministry initiatives, amazing growth almost always follows. The fact is we grow more in doing ministry than we do even from receiving ministry.

Fellowship. Fellowship with other believers (*koinonia*) occurs when believers share ministry, worship, and meals while learning to share their love of Christ with each other. There is an amazing dynamic that occurs when God's people assemble together in fellowship focused upon Christ and encouraging one another by "speaking the truth in love."

Evangelism. Sharing the gospel with others honors God and brings unparalleled joy into the life of the believer. When God uses us to bring others into the kingdom or to plant the seeds of the gospel, it unleashes joy in our hearts that is almost inexplicable, and it also causes joy in heaven: "There is joy before the angels of God over one sinner who repents" (Luke 15:10).

The sacraments. The Lord has given two sacraments to confirm the promises of the new covenant: baptism and the Lord's Supper. Baptism declares the death and resurrection of Christ, the believer's union with him, and the validity of God's covenant promises. The Lord's Supper ensures the believer's renewed focus on the gospel truth of Christ's atoning death and triumphant resurrection, and by doing so encourages both personal renewal and church revival.

Leadership Styles

As Christian leaders seeking to be shepherd leaders, servant leaders, and superintendent leaders who by God's grace effectively encourage, equip, and exhort the people of God, we will accomplish these dynamics through our own God-given personalities and sanctified use of our God-given gifts. So, what about styles of leadership? Life and leadership moments both demand different responses at different times by gifted and insightful leaders. Basically there are three identifiable styles of Bible-based leadership.

Authoritative Leadership

This style of leadership calls for *direct* orders to be given with clarity and with the expectation of immediate compliance. Discussion and consensus is not needed. The authoritative style is appropriate during an emergency when time is critical and when a trusted leader is placed in command. It was the style of leadership established by the elders at the Miami-area church where our team volunteered following Hurricane Andrew. The church leadership had placed a godly, capable, and trusted pastor in charge of a command post for helping the needy—and it was remarkably productive and efficient.

In a genuine emergency, decisive, responsive, and sacrificial leadership is absolutely appropriate, but it's a short-term leadership style. If it's prolonged after the crisis has passed, if it's misused or initiated unilaterally, it can produce resentment, confusion, and discouragement. Not only must the occasion demand the use of the authoritative style, trust in the leader is essential in its delivery. Leaders who have consistently cared for their people and have demonstrated sustained character and accessibility can assume authoritative leadership when the occasion demands it. Those who have failed to do so will experience disaster if they attempt to lead in an authoritative style no matter what the occasion might be. But, even when used appropriately, the authoritative style should be followed by a season of celebration and refreshment, which will allow renewal of the normal relationships between the leader and the people.

Participatory Leadership

Participatory leadership is superior to the authoritative style. It's especially effective for task-solving. It develops teamwork, it educates the leader, and it builds respect and encouragement. By developing teamwork, participatory leadership helps reproduce and multiply leaders. By involving others in the tasks, it allows the leader to benefit from the knowledge, insights, and experience of other team members. Granted, too much information-sharing can slow down task-solving and decision making, but a competent and responsible leader can manage that challenge. Participatory leadership also builds up team leaders by involving them and depending upon them. The leader and the other team members have the opportunity to develop mutual respect, which is an encouragement to everyone involved and usually not only elevates morale but leads to excellent decisions.

Delegated Leadership

The delegated style of leadership is the most effective for institutional settings and for long-term situations. It's Three-*D* leadership at its best. In order to delegate responsibility, a leader must define leadership, develop leaders, and deploy them. Delegation encourages individual team members to demonstrate ingenuity and initiative, which in turn helps develop new leaders. Delegation must *not* become an excuse to dump distasteful tasks on others. It must be sincerely designed to *define, develop,* and *deploy* new leaders according to their gifts, passions, and abilities. Christian leaders should never lead as "lone rangers." They should always have defined and developed leaders who can be deployed in their temporary or permanent absence, and this is best done by creating a team approach to leadership. The delegated style of leadership should be the norm within the church or an organization, and established leaders should habitually exercise it and mature in their implementation of it.[1]

Who is sufficient for these things? Not one of us. So it's time to pray: "Dear Lord, *please* make me a watchful shepherd, give me a servant's heart, and sustain me as a diligent superintendent. Please, Lord, enable me to lead like Christ—the Good Shepherd, the Suffering Servant, and Vigilant Superintendent. May my leadership be marked by the ways of your Word and not by the ways of the world. Amen."

Before the apostle Paul was called to glory, his final words declared, "I have fought the good fight . . ." (2 Tim. 4:7). The Christian life is a war. Our greatest need in leadership is not the corporate model of a CEO but those who know the victory of Christ in life and can lead their people from victory to victory for Christ. We need leaders who are not fearful of the battle but are strong and courageous. The army of the Lord awaits those who will lead us into the battle to fight the good fight. Our armor is sure. Our weapons are divinely designed. Now O Lord, where are our leaders?

11

FIGHTING THE GOOD FIGHT

"I have fought the good fight, . . .
I have kept the faith."

2 TIMOTHY 4:7

t's a war.

Sometimes we forget that—but we shouldn't. Scripture repeatedly instructs us that we Christians are engaged in ongoing spiritual warfare. That's another reason the church needs to abandon its singular fascinations with corporate models for leadership. Scripture does not emphasize business-style leadership models. On the other hand, there are numerous biblical allusions and illustrations and historical accounts of combat leadership. Scripture does not identify the church as a business, but it does describe the church as the "army of the LORD" as in Joshua 5:14. In Ephesians 6:13–16, the members of the church are advised to equip themselves with the "armor of God" and to "stand firm" with "the belt of truth, and . . . the breastplate of righteousness." Satan's "strongholds" are destroyed by "the weapons of our warfare," according to 2 Corinthians 10:4. And in Psalm 144:1, we're told: "Blessed be the LORD, my rock, who trains my hands for war, and my fingers for battle." We must never forget a central biblical revelation: the church has an adversary, a defeated but powerful enemy called Satan, who heads a demonic army in this world. And we're engaged in mortal combat with him.

Christian leaders should be taught what it means to follow the King into battle and lead his people "from victory to victory." Christian leaders must learn how to equip, inspire, and sustain the Lord's army. Spiritual warfare is waged with spiritual weapons, but that does not make it any less a war. Christian leaders must teach others how to be "soldiers of Christ"—and how to lead them. Do military metaphors and talk of war trouble you? If so, that's appropriate: spiritual warfare *is* troubling. But that doesn't mean you should remain ignorant and unprepared. Inspired by the Holy Spirit and on the eve of being called home, Paul summarized his life's ministry in 2 Timothy 4:7 with a metaphor of war: "I have fought the good fight, . . . I have kept the faith." Interpreted and instructed by the truth of Scripture, models of combat leadership are appropriate and useful. Let's examine some of them.

There are three types of combat leadership required for a victorious army: visionary leadership, which gives direction; strategic leadership, which gives a plan; and tactical leadership, which implements the plan. Seldom does any leader fit into a single type of combat leadership. Most leaders are a hybrid, and sometimes the combat at hand and the position of authority held by a leader dictate the type of leadership to be employed. Even so, most leaders are generally gifted in one type of leadership more than the others. Christian leadership is best advanced when leaders are trained to identify their own type of leadership (even if it is a hybrid) and then build teams of leaders that include all three types of combat leadership.

Visionary Leadership

When Imperial Japanese officers ended World War II with their official surrender in 1945, they did so aboard the battleship

USS *Missouri*—Fleet Admiral Chester W. Nimitz's flagship. The *Missouri* was an appropriate location for the surrender ceremony because Nimitz had provided much of the vision for American victory in the Pacific. After the Japanese surprise attack on Pearl Harbor in 1941, he was named commander of the U.S. Pacific Fleet—at least what was left of it. His assignment: lead the U.S. Navy from a humiliating defeat and destroy the Japanese empire. Nimitz played a key role in developing the American vision for victory and was then given responsibility for executing much of it. At the battles of Coral Sea and Midway, he inflicted a decisive combined defeat that stopped Japanese aggression and put the enemy on the defensive. It proved to be the turning point in the Pacific war. Never again would Imperial Japan hold so much of the world in its grasp.

Then, in joint operations with General Douglas MacArthur, Nimitz promoted a strategy that steadily drove Japanese forces back across an immense range of the Pacific Ocean. Instead of trying to assault and capture every Japanese stronghold on countless islands dotting the Pacific—an effort that would have seriously slowed the American advance—Nimitz developed a vision of "island hopping." American forces bypassed non-essential Japanese strongholds, leaving them to be "mopped up" later, and pressed forward to attack the Japanese mainland. When the Japanese surrendered on V-J Day, no one had done more to earn the victory than Admiral Nimitz. Although strategically and tactically implemented by others, it was his vision that triumphed over the evil that had oppressed Asia and the Pacific.

Visionary leaders such as Admiral Nimitz understand a mission's objectives and how to organize a team to achieve the mission's goals. They're able to visualize how the organization should function, what the team should do next, and what needs to be accomplished. They have the ability to see the *end* from the *beginning*—and keep the vision alive so that the team can always see the end. They know that a strategic plan and its tactical execution is crucial, so they strive to secure effective strategic and tactical leaders. The importance of visionary leadership is revealed with compelling frankness in the life of our Savior. The Great Commission establishes a vision of taking the gospel to the whole world. Our Lord enhances this vision when he tells us to "look . . . the fields are white for harvest." This visionary leadership provides direction. A visionary leader must first define the mission and then visualize its achievement. Then, the necessary organization, strategy, and goals can be established usually by using strategic and tactical leaders who own the mission and the vision. For Christian visionary leaders, this means ensuring that the team, the strategy, and the tactics are motivated, executed, and directed by faithful obedience to the Word of God. It is from God's Word that we are given the essentials, which ultimately define our mission and vision as Christian leaders.

Strategic Leadership

A strategic leader embraces a vision, develops a strategy to achieve the vision's goals, and oversees tactical leaders who implement the tactics necessary to produce a successful strategy. Strategic leaders embrace a visionary leader's direction, then devise and implement a strategy to successfully achieve it with an economy of resources. Visionary leaders tend to be immediately passionate about the vision, and are eager to share it. They may not have a strategic plan for implementing the vision, and most choose to delegate that crucial task to a strategic leader. The strategic leader creates an effective strategy that creates a pathway to victory and also develops the organizational structure required to implement the strategy, including a system to utilize or otherwise deal with criticism of the plan. A classic example of strategic leadership occurred during the American War for Independence at an obscure meadow in the Carolina backcountry—and it led directly to our American nationhood.

General George Washington's vision for victory in the American Revolution appeared dim in late 1780. Although American militia troops had won a key victory at the battle of King's Mountain in the South and long-awaited French reinforcements had arrived in the North, British forces had scored a series of victories and the American cause remained in peril. Washington's army was stalemated in New Jersey, some of his troops had organized a mutiny over lack of pay, and one of his most valued officers—General Benedict Arnold—had deserted to the enemy. British troops still occupied New York City, had resisted an attempted American advance onto Staten Island, and were mounting an aggressive Southern campaign in the Carolinas. In one of the worst American disasters of the war, the key port city of Charleston, South Carolina, had fallen to the British. Savannah was also in British hands, and a British army had inflicted a costly and humiliating defeat on American troops at the battle of Camden. The American cause desperately needed a victory to reverse the direction of the war—and it happened in the South Carolina backwoods, thanks to the strategic leadership of an American brigadier general named Daniel Morgan.

Morgan was an experienced Continental officer serving under the brilliant General Nathanael Greene, and was charged with helping turn back the British campaign to capture and occupy the Carolinas. In January 1781, Morgan found himself with an outnumbered army, penned against a flooded and impassable river, and facing a crack British army led by a ruthless commander named Banastre Tarleton. Yet Morgan's perilous position was by choice—it was a trap he intended to spring against the British. He knew that Lieutenant Colonel Tarleton favored rash frontal assaults, and he had intentionally deployed his troops to lure the British commander into combat. Morgan had strategically selected the field of battle—a sprawling, tree-lined pasture known as the Cowpens—and he intended to unleash a secret strategy on the British.

The night before the battle, Morgan moved among the camps of his small army, making speeches to his soldiers and encouraging them to do their best in the pending combat. When he finished, according to an eyewitness, his troops were "in good spirits and very willing to fight."[1] When the British attacked the next day, on the bitterly cold morning of January 17, 1781, Morgan had his army deployed in three lines: experienced and well-trained Continental regulars in the rear, volunteer militia troops in the center, and a force of hidden sharpshooters in the front. When the British came into range, marching forward in the frontal assault as Morgan had predicted, he gave an order and the sharpshooters opened fire on the British officers, eliminating much of the British leadership. The second line of militia, which had a reputation for firing a single volley and then fleeing, had promised Morgan that they would stand firm and fire two volleys before retreating. They did, and the British army charged after them—right into a surprise cavalry assault from their flanks. The well-trained British infantry took their losses and kept coming, but then saw the militia and the Continental regulars in their front turn and appear to flee. Without officers to control them, the British troops broke ranks and made an undisciplined charge. At Morgan's order, the American troops suddenly stopped their "retreat," turned, and fired volley after volley into the surprised British troops—and then followed up with a bold bayonet charge. The shock attack was too much for the British troops, who had few officers left to rally them, and their army disintegrated in a panicky rout.

The battle of Cowpens (which was the basis for the climactic battle in the motion picture *The Patriot*) was an overwhelming American victory, and came at a crucial time in the War for Independence. It launched a chain of military events in the South that eventually led to the British surrender at Yorktown and American independence—due in large part to the strategic leadership of Brigadier General Daniel Morgan. It was Washington's vision to defeat the British Southern campaign, but it was Morgan's strategy that advanced the vision. Washington—the commander-in-chief—was far away in New Jersey as his strategic victory occurred in South Carolina.

Tactical Leadership

Yet no battle is won by the visionary leader or the strategic leader; it's won by the soldier. And the soldier wins it with tactics: the methods and means of executing a strategic plan. That requires a tactical leader. A superb example of tactical leadership was established in World War I by a U.S. Marine Corps officer: Major General John A. Lejeune.

In the autumn of 1918, Allied forces—bolstered by the American Expeditionary Force—launched an offensive to drive German forces from the western front in France and Belgium. At the center of the advance in the French region of Champagne, French troops stalled against a powerful German stronghold called Blanc Mont Ridge, and the French commander turned to General Lejeune for assistance. Lejeune commanded the U.S. Second Division, a hard-fighting division of army and marine troops. A mixture of soldiers and marines in a single division might have proved troublesome to some commanders, but not to Lejeune, whose leadership had shaped the division into a highly regarded combat unit. At Blanc Mont Ridge, the French high command wanted to break up the Second Division and spread its men throughout the battle-weary French forces, which would have placed the Americans directly under French officers and would have eliminated the division's identity. Lejeune was outranked, but he adamantly urged his superiors not to break up his division—his men knew how to take Blanc Mont Ridge, and they would do it.

Reluctantly, the Allied commanders agreed to let him try. And the American soldiers and marines of the Second Division launched a mighty assault on the German stronghold on October 3, 1918. It was a bloody, two-hour uphill battle. Amid the fierce fighting, the supporting French troops faltered on both American flanks, causing Lejeune's men to draw blistering enemy machine-gun fire from both sides. They had been taught to fight, however, and they persevered, captured the ridge, and held it until finally reinforced. The Second Division assault on Blanc Mont Ridge spearheaded a sustained American drive that led to the Allied victory in World War I. So impressed were the French that they awarded two thousand Croix de Guerre medals to Lejeune's soldiers and marines, and presented Lejeune himself with the Legion of Honor. Back home, he was awarded the American Distinguished Service Cross and was promoted to commandant of the U.S. Marine Corps. Today, the Marine Corps' huge base in coastal North Carolina—Camp Lejeune—is named for this capable American tactical leader.

Tactical leaders embrace the vision shared by the visionary leader and the strategy shared by the strategic leader, and then provide the necessary leadership to equip, execute, and fulfill the plan by taking it from paper to the battlefield. They understand the training necessary to execute the plan, the organizational structure, and the deadlines that are required for success. They also know the strengths and weaknesses of their people. They can predict obstacles and establish contingency plans, so that those who are engaged in the effort will be able to adapt and overcome. Any strategic plan can be interrupted by an emergency, can falter because of poor communications, and can be damaged by uncontrollable events. Therefore, competent tactical leaders are extremely important. They must possess integrity, motivation, vigilance, flexibility, and decisiveness—the "on-site" skills that compose successful tactical leadership.

Again, leaders seldom fit perfectly into one of these types of leadership. When assembling a team of leaders, overall leadership should always be placed with someone who generally meets the definition of a visionary leader, which gives the team direction. Possessing and promoting the vision does not necessarily mean that team meetings should be led by a visionary. Some visionary leaders are not skillful discussion leaders, and in some cases organizational sessions are most effectively directed by the strategic leader. Sometimes the strategic leader focuses on developing a strategic plan, and leaves execution to the tactical leader. And sometimes a team has numerous tactical leaders, who each hold responsibility for some part of tactical execution, which in turn advances strategy and implements the vision.

Finally, it's vital for visionary, strategic, and tactical leaders to remember that success is ultimately achieved by the "troops" in the field: the people who successfully conduct the tasks that compose tactics, execute strategy, and transform the vision into reality. Major General Lejeune, for example, credited his troops with his victories, knowing (as does any wise leader) that successful leadership depends on the people you lead. He also knew the importance of inspired tactical leadership—the ability to convey the ultimate vision and its strategy to tactical execution by troops in the field. Soon after the armistice that ended World War I on November 11, 1918, Lejeune visited some of his wounded troops in a field hospital. One was a Marine Corps sergeant who had been severely wounded in an assault on a bridge in the fading hours of the war. Here's how Lejeune recalled the ultimate lesson in leadership that he learned from the wounded combat veteran:

> I asked him if he had heard before the battle that the Armistice would probably be signed within a few hours. He replied that it was a matter of common knowledge among the men. I then said, "What induced you to cross the bridge in the face of that terrible machine gun and artillery fire when you expected that the war would end in a few hours?" In answer, he said, "Just before we began to cross the bridge our battalion commander, Captain Dunbeck, assembled the companies around him in the ravine where we were waiting orders, and told us, 'Men, I am going across that river, and I expect you to go with me.'" The wounded man then remarked, "What could we do but go across too? Surely we couldn't let him go by himself; we love him too much for that." I have always felt that the incident I have just narrated gives one a better understanding of the meaning and the practice of leadership than do all the books that have been written, and all the speeches that have been made on the subject.[2]

Whether you are a visionary, strategic, or tactical leader—or a hybrid—be a selfless leader who inspires your followers by going anywhere and doing anything that you expect of them. It's not just military tradition. It's the biblical model of leadership.

Now, having defined leaders and leadership, how do you develop them? How can at least part of the disciple making ministry of the church start producing leaders so that the church becomes a leadership factory not only for itself but also for the world?

12

THE CHURCH AS A LEADERSHIP FACTORY AND DISTRIBUTION CENTER

"He is very useful to me for ministry."
2 TIMOTHY 4:11

He's alive!

The news raced through Jerusalem that Jesus of Nazareth—crucified on Golgotha, dead, and buried—was now alive, and eyewitnesses had verified the reports. He had risen from the dead, appeared to more than five hundred of his followers, and had ascended to heaven amidst a cloud of glory. Already Jesus—Y'shua Messiah, the Christ—was causing an even greater impact through his death, resurrection, and ascension than he did in life. Thousands were coming to Christ. The historical narrative of this kingdom movement of the gospel is found in the book of Acts. The second chapter of Acts describes the lifestyle of the church and the new believers—how they loved to hear God's Word, loved to worship, loved to pray, and loved to give. It also records the amazing proliferation of leaders who were produced by the leaders that Christ had trained—the apostles.

The Church's First Leaders

One of these converts—Joseph of Cypress—became so well known for his sacrificial giving and gift of encouragement that his name was changed, according to Acts 4:36. Instead of calling him *Joseph*, the believers came to call him *Barnabas—Bar* meaning "son of" and *nabas* meaning "encouragement." The old Joseph became the new "son of encouragement" because the grace of God had given him a new heart manifested by sacrificial giving and encouragement.

Another dramatic conversion came to a religious terrorist named Saul, who had persecuted, imprisoned, and killed Christians in the mistaken notion that he was serving God. Initially after his conversion he was shunned by the apostles because they feared and mistrusted him, but another believer—this man named Barnabas—defended Saul and discipled him. A few years later, after God had blessed Barnabas with a ministry beyond his capacity in Antioch, he sent for Saul, whom he helped develop as a leader, preacher, and teacher. Directed by the Holy Spirit, the church at Antioch dispatched Barnabas and Saul on a mission trip, which became known as the "first missionary journey." Scripture identifies them as Barnabas and Saul, and the order of their names indicates that Saul was still under the tutelage of Barnabas. Yet by the time they returned, Saul, too, had undergone a name change. He had become *Paul*, which means "small" in Greek and accordingly humbly emphasized his description of himself as "the least of the apostles." By the end of the first missionary journey, the name order had also shifted. Instead of "Barnabas and Saul," it had become "Paul and Barnabas."

The apostles who had been trained by Christ as leaders multiplied themselves, and Barnabas, one of the new leaders, had multiplied himself by developing Paul as a leader. He was so effective and successful that eventually Paul became his leader. Someone who performs in a large symphony once told me that the hardest position to fill in the orchestra is second-chair violinist. No one wants to play "second fiddle." But if Barnabas struggled with the sin of pride, he conquered it in Christ because he developed leaders so successfully that they even went beyond him in ministry effectiveness. He apparently and amazingly moved willingly from the premier position in ministry on the first missionary journey to the new status of "second fiddle"—presumably mindful of the biblical admonition that the "last shall be first." Acts 15 reports that Paul suggested taking a second missionary journey with Barnabas. Although Barnabas felt led to go, he wished to make his cousin John Mark part of the missionary team. Paul rejected the idea because he anticipated that young John Mark would quit as he had on the first missionary journey. But Barnabas wanted to give Mark another chance—remember he is the encourager—because he saw his potential as a leader. Paul disagreed sharply because he was developing a team of proven leaders, not potential leaders for the specific task at hand.

The result was that John Mark made a mission trip with Barnabas, and Paul took Silas, so both Mark and Silas were tutored by multiplying leaders. Interestingly, Mark was equipped and matured as a leader under Barnabas and later became a crucial member of Peter's ministry team. Peter acknowledged Mark's maturity and his relationship with him in 1 Peter 5:13, referring to Mark as "my son." Paul also acknowledged Mark's growth from a potential leader to a proven leader in Colossians 4:10, advising the letter's primary readers to open their hearts and homes to "Mark the cousin of Barnabas (concerning whom you have received instructions—if he comes to you, welcome him)." Furthermore, at the end of his life, Paul demonstrated his respect and dependence on Mark by calling for his presence because he was "very useful to me for ministry" (2 Tim. 4:11).

The Jesus Model

Inspired by the Holy Spirit, Paul outlined the biblical concept of multiplication leadership at the end of his life in his final letter to Timothy:

You then, my child, be strengthened by the grace that is in Christ Jesus, and what you have heard from me in the presence of many witnesses entrust to faithful men who will be able to teach others also." (2 Tim. 2:1–2)

This passage clearly sets forth the method of implementing the Three-*D* biblical principle of leadership production: leaders should be *defined, developed,* and *deployed.* The Lord had previously demonstrated the same principle in his three-year-long earthly ministry. In the "Jesus Model"—which was followed by Barnabas, Paul, and other New Testament leaders—a principal leader multiplies himself, developing proven leaders from potential leaders, who then attract possible leaders.

Diagram 12.1 The Biblical Model of Leadership Multiplication

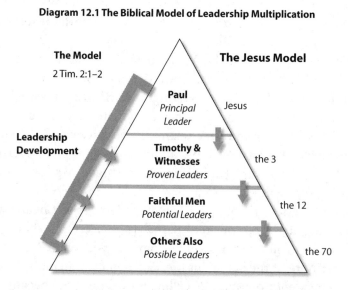

The biblical model of leadership—which is so clearly delineated in 2 Timothy 2:1–2—called Timothy to imitate Paul just as Paul imitated Christ. Paul was the *principal* leader. He invested himself in Timothy, who was the *proven* leader, according to Philippians 2:22: "But you know Timothy's proven worth, how as a son with a father he has served with me in the gospel." Other proven leaders were apparently learning along with Timothy, according to

2 Timothy 2:1–2, to whom Paul refers with the statement: "what you have heard from me in the presence of many witnesses." We know some of these other proven leaders: Aquilla and Pricilla, Silas, Titus, Luke, etc.

As a proven leader, Timothy in turn helped develop *potential* leaders, who are profiled as "faithful men who will be able to teach others also." Notice the two distinctive marks of potential leaders in this passage. First, potential leaders should be consistent in faith and practice to the point of being called "faithful." Second, they should be willing to exercise multiplication by conducting their ministry through a team of *possible* leaders, who are called "others" in the text. In 2 Timothy 2:1–2, Paul is also affirming that the church's ministry is best done through teams. The *principal* leader is the pastor, who should invest in a team of *proven* leaders (i.e., ordained officers and staff), who each in turn conduct ministry through teams of *potential* leaders, who each then develop ministry teams of *possible* leaders (others).

Finally, ministry through teams of leaders must be a non-negotiable commitment so that every leader is on a team and does ministry through a team of leaders, who also each lead teams. When ministry is carried out through teams of leaders, there are extraordinary benefits and blessings. For instance, if more *proven* leaders are needed, team ministry will develop them through training and experience. Likewise, *potential* and *possible* leaders will continually surface through ministry endeavors. Team ministry also provides nurture, accountability, and encouragement as well as multiple insights and sources of wisdom. Three-*D* leadership in the church—*defining, developing,* and *deploying* leaders—depends greatly on a pastor who delights in developing new leaders and sharing leadership through an intentional commitment to doing ministry through teams of leaders. Under the Lord, the pastor as the *principal* leader must first develop a team of *proven* leaders who are committed to further the ministry by developing *potential* leaders, each of whom can commit to conducting ministry with a team of *possible* leaders. Leadership formation thus occurs throughout the entire ministry infrastructure just as it did in the New Testament church. The result is the church again reclaiming the opportunity to be a leadership factory and distribution center affecting families, communities, and the entire culture.

How can the pastor of a local church implement the principle of team ministry and therefore multiplication of leadership? Here are some suggestions:

- Teach the biblical principle of leadership from 2 Timothy 2:1–2.
- Establish the non-negotiable precedent of conducting ministry through teams of leaders and declare that every leader is to be on a team and every leader must do his ministry through a team.
- Recruit a team of *proven* leaders, who each will commit to recruiting a team of *potential* leaders who each will commit to recruiting *possible* leaders.
- Apply the biblical principle of leadership through teams to all areas of ministry in the church.
- Obtain a commitment from the formal church leaders that ministry will always be performed in teams and that the goal of each team will include developing leaders as well as achieving ministry.
- Take the lead in communicating the pivotal point that existing leadership should always develop "teams of leaders" rather than "leadership teams." Leadership teams tend to become the servants of the leader of the team, but if you develop a team of leaders, those leaders will not only develop teams of leaders but the pastor will have to become a servant to them for their success as a leader of leaders. Developing teams of leaders produces the blessing of multiplying leadership and the joy of allowing the *principal* leader to become the servant of the team of leaders.

Under this biblical paradigm of leadership development, new leaders will inevitably "bubble up" from the inside. This ministry infrastructure of teams of leaders will generate leaders internally who have been discipled by knowledgeable Christian leaders instead of depending upon recruiting leaders externally who have been discipled by the world. Then the church will be a leadership factory not only for the church itself but also for the family and every sphere of society. The church multiplying leaders will impact families, neighborhoods, businesses, and the surrounding community. Of course, it will not stop there—praise the Lord—but will even be used to send the gospel to all the nations of the world.

Sound like the Great Commission? It is. And it will shake the world.

13

IF IT AIN'T HORSE, CARVE IT OUT!

"Take my instruction instead of silver,
and knowledge rather than choice gold. . . ."
PROVERBS 8:10

It's not about counting numbers; it's about the caliber of leaders.

Many people believe that effective leadership is measured by a large following. If that were true, we'd have to respect some of the world's worst evils, such as communism and fascism. Not to mention the billions of people who have been misled by counterfeit religions. Granted, lack of numerical growth *can* be an indication of something wrong somewhere. A large following, however, does not necessarily reflect the presence of biblical leadership. A truer test of an effective Bible-based leader lies not with the size of the followership, but with the quality of leaders he produces. It's quality of leaders not quantity of followers. Effective biblical leadership normally does produce multiplication and growth—the same way that rivulets become brooks, brooks become creeks, creeks become streams, and streams become mighty rivers. It's a process. Usually it requires the passage of time. Ministry movements can and have been produced in a moment of time, but usually the movements of God's kingdom arise as he calls multiplication leaders who are developed over a period of time. When the biblical paradigm of leadership development is faithfully applied, leaders multiply, and so do followers as a consequence. But remember, this process begins with genuine biblical leadership. For three years Christ *defined* leadership, *developed* leaders, and *deployed* them with the mission and vision of the Great Commission along with the power of the Holy Spirit. The result was the unstoppable movement of the kingdom of God, which is still expanding in this world for God's glory.

All truth is God's truth. An abundance of leadership instruction is available in contemporary American culture—maybe an overabundance. Some of it contains a lot of truth, some little, and some none. Where truth exists, however, it's God's truth, and you can be sure that God was there first. I've studied much of the literature on leadership—both secular and Christian—and by the grace of God, I'm convinced that what's honorable and true in all of it was found first in the Word of God. How do secular people discover and use God's truth? By what we call "common grace." God allows unbelievers by his grace and mercy to understand and implement that which is true and good even though they may use it for their own purposes and not for his glory. Based on God's truth revealed in his Word and what I've learned from the study of leadership literature, five important habits common to biblical leadership that intentionally reproduces have surfaced with astounding clarity. These five habits are absolutely crucial to being a multiplication leader and to the vision of reclaiming the church as a leadership factory and distribution center.[1]

A Leader Is an Insatiable Learner

Biblical leaders have a hunger to learn. It's an almost unquenchable drive, and it's biblical. Scripture instructs us that we are to seek wisdom—and remember that wisdom begins with the proper fear of God. From that foundation, we are to grow in our knowledge of the Lord, his Word, his ways, and the world he created. A God-centered search for wisdom and knowledge honors the Lord, and it's as old as his creation. "The LORD possessed me [wisdom] at the beginning of his work, the first of his acts of old. Ages ago I [wisdom] was set up, at the first, before the beginning of the earth" (Prov. 8:22–23). That quest for wisdom and knowledge can be a useful tool for the Lord's work and his glory when it's God-centered. "Take my instruction instead of silver," advises Proverbs 8:10, "and knowledge rather than choice gold. . . ."

God doesn't want us to squander our time on knowledge for knowledge's sake. That dishonors him and makes the pursuit of knowledge idolatry. It's easy to embrace the idol of knowledge in our information age. Pleasure reading. Using the Internet. Watching television, motion pictures, documentaries. All can be useful and at times recreationally restful—if our approach to them is God-centered. But to maximize leadership learning, we need discipline. And don't make the mistake of leaning just on what you have already learned, which is evidence of personal arrogance. Such prideful neglect of learning inevitably produces lazy and ineffective leaders. Don't be too busy to keep learning. *Great leaders are great learners.* The old adage is true: "Don't put the urgent before the important." And while you seek to know all about it, don't be a know-it-all.

Was Jesus a learner? Absolutely: "And Jesus increased in wisdom, and in stature, and in favor with God and man" (Luke 2:52). Jesus was fully God and therefore omniscient as God the Son, but he was also fully man. And as the Son of Man he intentionally "increased in wisdom." So as a biblical leader, you should seek to fulfill your hunger to learn and do so joyfully and with anticipation of how what you are learning will increase your ability to honor the Lord as a Christian leader. Obviously, study and research—even of Christian works—should not replace your personal time in the Word of God. As you organize a plan for ongoing learning, you'll want to apply your personal learning style. For instance, you may include formal classroom study and small group discussion sessions to your growth plan, or you may find articles, audio programs, or films useful. But remember that most serious research is based upon book-length treatments of subject matter. Here are some suggestions for a disciplined categorical foundation for continued learning:

- Commentaries, language tools, and theological journals
- Biographies and histories
- Apologetics and evangelism
- Periodicals
- Devotional commentaries and books
- Communication and/or leadership works
- Contemporary issues, politics, cultural developments
- Regularly scheduled conferences and retreats thoughtfully selected
- An annual sabbatical (one to four weeks) for study, meditation, reflection, writing, prayer, and fasting—formally planned, structured with accountability, and *not* a substitute for a family vacation. (My sabbatical is three weeks in length with identifiable objectives and a report at its conclusion that is given to the elders.)

Leaders Seize the Learning Moment

There are special moments in life when we are especially teachable. Often the hardest times teach us the most memorable lessons. That fact is taught in Scripture and affirmed by personal experience. Adversity, failure, challenges, disappointments, and suffering all hold severe mercies—treasures of wisdom for those who are humble enough to be teachable in tough times. "Count it all joy, my brothers, when you meet trials of various kinds, for you know that the testing of your faith produces steadfastness. And let steadfastness have its full effect, that you may be perfect and complete, lacking in nothing" (James 1:2–4). That crucial truth is driven home in Romans 5:3–4: "More than that, we rejoice in our sufferings, knowing that suffering produces endurance, and endurance produces character, and character produces hope. . . ." When yielded to the Lord, even and especially when they're self-inflicted, the hardships of life can be transformed by God to teach us, bless us, and grow us in righteousness.

One of the challenges of learning from those special, difficult teaching moments is that they're also the moments when we're most apt to engage in self-preservation and self-pity. We must be careful that our tendency toward self-protection in those hard moments doesn't block us from learning God's appointed lessons. Seldom do we learn in times of affluence and prosperity. "God whispers to us in our pleasures . . . but shouts to us in our pains," wrote C. S. Lewis in *The Problem of Pain*.[2] Adversity yielded to the Lord can open the vaults of wisdom if you choose to enter boldly and not retreat fearfully. Do not miss the moment by retreating into self-pity or self-preservation, by blaming others, or by embracing anger or bitterness. Instead, seize the moment, as painful as it may be, and realize that the Lord has just rung the school bell. Class is in. There are great lessons to learn. Learn them well. The wife of Jonathan Edwards, in a letter to her daughter after the untimely death of her husband who had just become the president of the College of New Jersey (now Princeton University), provides a remarkable testimony of how God's grace enables us to learn even in our deepest moments of grief and adversity:

> My very dear child, What shall I say! A holy and good God has covered us with a dark cloud. O that we may kiss the rod, and lay our hands upon our mouths! The Lord has done it. He has made me adore his goodness, that we had [your father] so long. But my God lives; and he has my heart. O what a legacy my husband, and your father, has left us! We are all given to God; and there I am, and love to be. Your affectionate mother, Sarah Edwards.[3]

Leaders Lead Others to Learn

A biblical leader thrives on giving away what has been learned by teaching and coaching others. Leaders should enthusiastically recruit and assemble their team of leaders, train them, and put them to work—and then stand ready to encourage, instruct, disciple, and embrace as needed. Great leaders are not only insatiable learners, they are unstoppable teachers, insistently coaching and taking great joy when they see their disciples walking in the truth. Being a leader who continually teaches and coaches others can be excruciatingly difficult. It can be discouraging. It can be thankless. It can even be dangerous. And it is often exhausting—but it produces an exhilarating joy even at the moment of exhaustion. The scriptural truth that "it is more blessed to give than to receive" (Acts 20:35) is continually affirmed through God-centered, Bible-based leadership.

When it's hard, avoid complaining—but don't fake it. You don't have to wear a grin all the time or be "professionally" upbeat. Mentoring is often hard; just don't make it unnecessarily so. Embrace the joy of the Lord in the gift of being a leader/coach. Savor it gratefully. And when it's appropriate—which is often—demonstrate the joy of your salvation and the pleasure of serving the risen Christ Jesus by equipping the next generation of leaders. "A glad heart makes a cheerful face," observes Proverbs 15, which also clearly states that "the cheerful of heart has a continual feast" (Prov. 15:13, 15). If you grow weary or dreary, step back from the fray and go to the Lord for a period of refreshment, healing, and redirection. Make it your daily goal to exercise an attitude of gratitude and to seek the contentment and fulfillment that come from a surrendered and obedient heart. Learn to love leadership. Remember, you can't give away what you don't know. You have known the joy of being a learner, the discipline of seizing your personal learning moments, and the inexplicable joy of giving it away to others as a mentor and coach. So let's stop, take a moment, and give praise to God. You have not only been gifted but you have been made a gift to others. Now, the last two habits are crucial to making you effective as a multiplication leader.

Leaders Use Memorable Maxims

"Remember who you are and where you are from." I can still hear those words a generation later, just as they were delivered by my high school principal. He was a remarkable leader. He seemed to know the name of every student—almost two thousand of us—and he regularly greeted each one of us that way. He led a well-run, highly effective public high school, and he did it with a character-based honor code. No locks were permitted on student lockers; the honor code prevented theft. Teachers left the classroom during testing; the honor code prevented cheating. Nobody would have dared to seriously attack another student; the honor code prevented violence. The principal kept the standards high, and one effective tool he used was memorable maxims. I remember several, but the one that he used as a foundation for everything else called on us to conduct ourselves in a manner that upheld a good name and honored our families and our school: "Remember who you are and where you are from." At our fortieth reunion the first thing out of our mouths to each other was that simple statement. A truly memorable maxim. As a result, our student body pursued living up to that expectation and nobody wanted to undermine it, thanks to the leadership of our principal and the use of a memorable maxim.

Decades later, I visited the same school, and I was shocked. Not only were locks affixed to every locker, but all the doors were locked and equipped with alarms. Police officers patrolled the halls. Instead of the blessings of a self-regulated honor code, the students were basically imprisoned to protect them from one another. The dramatic change was sobering evidence of how our nation had abandoned its foundational perspective: a biblical worldview that created an ethical perspective on life that included the words of our high school principal, which called us to integrity, sobriety, honesty, and simply loving others as you would have them love you. In a word, that was the foundation of our honor code. Today's leaders have failed us. Our nation has turned from the Lord, and within a single generation the rotten fruit of that rebellion was glaringly obvious in the walls of a public high school. Knowing what the Bible says about sin, that does not amaze me. But what saddens me is that we are no longer producing leaders with a Christian world- and life-view who are deployed into the spheres of our society, including the halls of education. As I made a heartsick appraisal of my old school, I remember thinking: *Everything rises and falls on leadership.*

At home, church, school, work, and everywhere, biblical leaders must teach that character indeed does count. And a priceless tool for driving home the appropriate lessons is a memorable maxim. Did Jesus do that? Did he teach with memorable maxims? Absolutely. Look at the Gospels, and you'll see thirty-two parables, two allegories, six sermons, and countless meaningful observations used by the Lord to teach his followers and us— memorable maxims all. You can do it, too. It's simply a matter of taking a profound truth and reducing it to a statement that's easy to remember. Pray about it and do it. If you want to effectively exercise biblical leadership, develop the habit of teaching with clear, simple, and memorable maxims. They can last—and work—for a lifetime.

Leaders Show Disciples How to Seize Learning Moments

A biblical leader not only seizes his own learning moments, but also helps his disciples learn how to do the same. Leaders embrace, encourage, comfort, instruct—and also insist on the discipline of learning and capturing the learning moments. As in parenting, the application of discipline for learning is usually the most challenging. But it's also vital. When I was a boy, my dad would occasionally take me for a walk with him. Sometimes as we walked together, he would playfully swing his leg to the side and give me a light kick on the seat of my pants. It always took me by surprise, and I couldn't figure out how he could swing his leg around while walking, but I could not wait until I was a dad and could do the same thing. What I didn't know was that my dad was actually giving me an experience that profiles ministry.

As I walked along with him, his arm around my shoulder, security and comfort were assured—but then came "the kick."

When people experience moments of adversity, failure, and disappointment, our arm must be around them for verbal and physical comfort and encouragement, but at the right time there needs to be a kick in the pants by inquiring, "What is God trying to teach you? The school bell has just rung and you are in God's classroom so let's not waste the moment but seize it as a learning moment." That's what the discipline of learning is to those we lead and love. When someone is hurting, confused, frustrated, even angry, a Christian leader's rightful inclination is to provide comfort—especially if the leader is a pastor. The importance of following that biblically based inclination cannot be overemphasized. But neither can the importance of simultaneously implementing or overseeing the discipline of learning. It, too, is an act of love, and often can be even more productive than a hug, a financial gift, or well-spoken words of encouragement. Remember Hebrews 12:11: "For the moment all discipline seems painful rather than pleasant, but later it yields the peaceful fruit of righteousness to those who have been trained by it." If you love those you lead, you will gently but firmly direct the discipline of learning when it's appropriate. And you'll stand ready to help them identify and seize other kinds of learning moments when they come. Remember, adversity is usually a providentially divine appointment for learning.

Did Jesus assist his disciples in seizing their personal learning moments? Yes, he did, and the Gospels are replete with examples. Studying the apostle Peter's relationship with the Lord reveals numerous occasions when Jesus assisted Peter in defining and seizing a personal learning moment. Perhaps the most memorable example occurred after Christ's resurrection. Remember how—in the dark, dangerous hours before the crucifixion—Peter had denied the Lord three times? After the resurrection, alive and risen from the dead, Jesus gently confronted Simon Peter on the banks of the Sea of Galilee. The event is reported in John 21:15–18: "Simon, son of John," Jesus asked, "do you love me more than these?" Jesus likely gestured toward the other disciples as he asked the question because Peter had boasted that even if they deserted the Lord, he would not. "Yes, Lord; you know that I love you," Peter affirmed. "Feed my lambs," Jesus told him, and then asked the question a second time. Peter gave the same answer: "Yes, Lord; you know that I love you." Jesus replied, "Tend my sheep," and then repeated the question a third time—"Simon, son of John, do you love me?" Peter was grieved to be asked three times to profess his love. "Lord, you know everything," he said; "you know that I love you." Again Jesus said to him, "Feed my sheep."

What was going on? A deeper study of the original Greek words for *love* reveals a marvelous point, but the main lesson here deals with Peter's threefold denial. Clearly, Jesus was challenging Peter to seize a crucial learning moment. He had publicly denied Christ three times, and Jesus here allowed Peter to affirm him three times. The old had gone, the new had come—and Peter experienced the blessing of forgiveness and a new beginning. Do you think Peter ever forgot that learning moment? It was a painful, humbling experience for him, but it was a learning moment that left him better equipped as a Christian leader. No wonder that when Peter challenges the leaders of the church in 1 Peter 5:1–11, he reminds them that "God opposes the proud but gives grace to the humble. Humble yourselves, therefore, under the mighty hand of God so that at the proper time he may exalt you" (1 Pet. 5:5–6). The next time Peter is recorded as speaking publicly is when he stands before thousands as he preaches the gospel, and more than three thousand people come to Jesus Christ as Lord and Savior. The Lord breaks those whom he is going to use so that it is his strength in which we boast and not our own. If that is true of believers, it is certainly true of leaders.

Summary

When faithfully followed, these five habits of biblical leadership can dramatically shape a leader's life and position him to be a multiplication leader as a vital instrument in the Lord's church as it pursues the opportunity to be a leadership factory and distribution center. Scripture commands us—leaders as well as followers—to constantly be seeking to grow in the Lord, to live and to lead for him. "I have been crucified with Christ," wrote Paul in Galatians 2:20. "It is no longer I who live, but Christ who lives in me. And the life I now live in the flesh I live by faith in the Son of God, who loved me and gave himself for me."

Did you ever read about the New York City reporter who traveled to Virginia's Blue Ridge Mountains to interview an acclaimed wood-carver? The old mountaineer carved exquisite horse models, and his craftsmanship had somehow been discovered by the national media. The reporter tracked down the mountain woodworker and examined his art: extraordinary carved horses rendered from solid blocks of oak. The creations were stunningly beautiful. Their hooves appeared as if suspended in midair, and their manes looked as if they were flowing in the wind. "How do you do it?" the reporter questioned the old man. "How do you carve such magnificent, lifelike creations from solid blocks of oak?" "I don't know, son," the mountaineer replied. "I just do it." Determined to learn the old man's technique, the reporter pried more. "What's the full story? What is your secret?" "Sonny, it's no secret," the craftsman finally explained. "I just get my carving knife and a nice block of oak wood, and I carve out everything that ain't horse."

Lord, please carve away everything in our lives that ain't Jesus.

14

WHO IS ON THE TEAM?

*"And he went up on the mountain
and called to him those whom he desired,
and they came to him."*

MARK 3:13

D on't try to be the Lone Ranger.

It takes teamwork. A carefully and prayerfully selected team of leaders is essential. It's the biblical model of leadership, and furthermore it works. Remember, a principal leader defines, develops, and deploys proven leaders, who develop potential leaders, who in turn develop possible leaders. Therefore, selecting leaders is vitally important—but how is it best done?

Pinpointing Leaders

Recruiting a team of leaders requires prayer, care, and wisdom. The obvious first step is to establish criteria for identifying leaders for the team. Let's call that criteria the "Six Cs"—calling, character, content, competency, commitment, and chemistry.

Calling

Leaders must have a calling. They should have prayerfully evaluated their calling to ministry leadership—meaning that they realize the Lord has called them to lead and they're willing to pay the price of leadership out of love to him. They should also understand that while salvation is free, discipleship will cost, and leadership will cost even more. Furthermore, they should be recognized as leaders by others—meaning that they've surrendered to God's internal calling to leadership and have confirmed that calling through evaluation, affirmation, and recognition by others.

Character

Again, character is key. Before anyone is granted the privilege of occupying the position of leader, his personal character and conduct must be affirmed. Every Christian has a spiritual gift for ministry, and every Christian is fully saved from all his or her sins. Yet not everyone is qualified to be a leader. Those who are called to leadership are held to a higher standard: "Not many of you should become teachers, my brothers, for you know that we who teach will be judged with greater strictness" (James 3:1). Leaders "must be above reproach," and it's the responsibility of oversight leadership to ensure that leaders possess consistent character before they are deployed. Not only must a leader be qualified but a leader can also be disqualified through careless conduct and sinful lifestyle decisions. Remember, leadership is a privilege that is not attached to the fact that you are a Christian but is bestowed by recognition of your calling and consistent progress in the grace of God as a follower of Christ.

Content

Leaders should "know their stuff." First, they should be rooted and grounded in the Word of God and should know what it means to be a follower of Christ with a loving commitment to biblical integrity. Next, they should know their stuff when it comes to principled Christian leadership, and they should know their stuff in their area of expertise. If they lead a worship team, they should know worship. If they lead an administrative team, they should know administration. If they lead an outreach team, they should know evangelism. And in whatever ministry to which they're called, they also should know how to reproduce and multiply themselves through their own ministry team of leaders. But remember, most of all, they must know the Word of God in order to know the God of the Word and therefore how to serve the Lord as a leader among the people of God.

Competency

Calling, character, and content are delivered through leadership competencies. Proven leaders not only should "know their stuff" but must also be competent in the skills required to accomplish their ministry for the Lord. They should have acquired the skills necessary to accomplish their particular mission and ministry. Moreover, they should continue to improve those skills and acquire others as needed. Not only is competency necessary for efficient exercise of leadership, it also simultaneously encourages and provides comfort to those who are in the care of the leader as they are increasingly aware that their leader not only knows what to do but by God's grace is able to competently achieve it.

Commitment

Just as Paul advised Timothy to "fulfill [the] ministry" to which he had been called in 2 Timothy 4:5, so, too, do modern leaders need unwavering commitment. The objective of a leader is not self-fulfillment but self-sacrifice to achieve ministry fulfillment. That, of course, is what's really fulfilling personally. To be "poured out as a drink offering," as Paul proclaimed in 2 Timothy 4:6, may be all consuming but it is also exceedingly fulfilling.

Chemistry

Finally, there's chemistry. Leaders must learn how to work as a team, which obviously requires teamwork, and teamwork requires chemistry in relationships and performance. Chemistry is one of the greatest challenges facing a leader when building a team of leaders. In the hands of a competent and committed chemist, combining elements to achieve a necessary compound is not a mystery. But leadership chemistry is much more of an art than a science. Assembling a team of leaders with appropriate chemistry can be reasonably ensured by requiring an affirmative answer from the team members to three questions:

- Does each team member comprehend and embrace the ministry vision and its goals?
- Does each team member recognize and personally commit to support the leader of the team of leaders?
- Will each team member commit to developing and sustaining meaningful and supportive relationships with others on the team of leaders?

If you are placed in the position of interviewing a leadership candidate, never give in to the temptation to manipulate an affirmative answer to any of the above questions. Never go unprepared into an interview with a leadership candidate. Always be responsible to the ministry and the candidate by thoroughly examining every reference and securing secondary references. When interviewing a leadership candidate, be pleasant, of course, but be serious—not casual or informal. Being on a team of Christian leaders is never a frivolous issue. Don't downplay the costs of leadership. Don't promote, recruit, or "sell"; instead, provide ample information and a frank assessment of the responsibilities and challenges as well as the opportunities. It's also essential to allow the candidate time for prayer and reflection before accepting the position on the team of leaders. So even if these questions are answered affirmatively, avoid pushing the candidate to immediately accept the position offered. A follow-up interview is usually prudent. When the principal leader, proven leaders, potential leaders, and possible leaders faithfully affirm these questions, a team of leaders is well on its way to functioning effectively with genuine and productive chemistry.

Prayer, Counsel, and Change

An authentic *calling*, consistent *character*, informative *content*, demonstrated *competency*, true *commitment*, and productive *chemistry* are powerful team dynamics when applied as gifts of God's grace from Christ through the Holy Spirit. But to apply them requires prayer and the insights of wise counselors. Remember, a Christian leader should not only pray for the work of the ministry but realize that prayer *is* the work of the ministry. Nothing else we do is more important than intercessory prayer for leaders and leadership. Develop a team of leaders that makes prayer a priority. For leaders, prayer precedes leadership, permeates leadership, and follows the efforts of leadership. We have not because we ask not (James 4:3).

And do not fail to seek the insights of wise counselors. Proverbs 15:22 tells us that there is wisdom in many counselors. The quantity of counselors may be relative—two counselors may be "many" in some situations; several or more may be "many" in others—but Scripture repeatedly emphasizes the quality of counsel: it must be "wise." Wise counsel is biblical, and biblical counsel flows most readily from those who are walking with the Lord faithfully and consistently. Seek such spiritually mature counselors and listen to their counsel, always testing everything by the Word of God.

When is a change in the team of leaders appropriate? If it is appropriate, how do you implement it? The brief answer is that you always make changes following biblical precepts and guidelines. If a leadership team is unable to achieve the mission, then either the mission is wrong and needs to be reconsidered or the right team is not in place and needs to be re-formed. It's possible that both may be true, but usually it is one or the other. The team mission may need to adjust. If so, then prayerful patience will be needed as the mission is reexamined. It is always appropriate to examine the mission or the leadership team to be certain that everything is biblical, God-centered, and strategically appropriate. Has the ministry become man-centered or

163

man-directed? If so, there is the need to not only refocus and re-form but also to repent. "But seek first the kingdom of God and his righteousness," Matthew 6:33 promises us, "and all these things will be added to you."

If you're the principal leader, you should first prayerfully examine yourself before the Lord. Have you contributed to the lack of success? If so, you should assume responsibility, make changes, or even resign. If the problem is the composition of the team, does a personnel change need to be made? Whenever I am praying about a change of personnel on the team of leaders, I always ask myself two questions about the individual under consideration to determine if I am on the right track. (1) If that individual resigned, would I be glad? If so, either my heart is not right toward that team member or that person should probably not be on the team. (2) If that position were vacant, would I fill it with the individual who currently occupies it? If not—and my heart is right—then that person should probably not be on the team in that position.

So if a change really is needed, how do you as the principal leader of the team of leaders bring it about? First, rather than focusing on removing someone, you should focus on helping the individual in question find where God wants him or her to be. Your first effort is to assist him or her in finding a right fit for his or her leadership abilities, style, and passion. You don't fix blame; you fix the problem. Often that means applying gifts and talents where they really belong. In other words, find the right team that fits people's leadership abilities. But, be careful: don't try to invent a job that fits the individual—that is usually a poor short-term solution and brings about other problems at a later date.

Sometimes when personnel changes are needed on the team, personal confession and repentance are required, as well as reciprocal forgiveness. The team of leaders will not experience God's full blessing if serious issues are ignored and sin is covered instead of confessed. If, after prayer and wise counsel, the team member in question still resists the change, or if the change produces bitterness and resentment that affect the team, the entire team may need to become involved. Any conflict in a church ministry should be biblically resolved by the church leadership authority. In a parachurch ministry, resolution is usually the responsibility of the ministry's oversight board. Of course, the key text that guides resolution and reconciliation for all Christians, including Christian leaders, is Matthew 18:15–18. (If outside counsel or resolution is required, I heartily recommend Peacemaker Ministries [www. peacemaker.net], which offers guidance in biblical conflict resolution and in creating a culture of peace in an organization.)

Team Vitality and Energy

So you have a team of leaders. How can you enhance the team's performance? How can you elevate the energy and motivation of the team? First, remember that teams are like people. The energy level rises and falls for a variety of reasons during the seasons of life. Teams are no different. Just as our bodies need rest, nourishment, and exercise in order to be energized, leadership teams need sources of energy. Here are five energy sources that elevate a team's ability to perform with vitality.

Embrace the Team Leader. The team leader brings passion, excitement, expertise, and energy for the team vision and mission. The team leader's energy and passion are contagious, but only if the team leader is *embraced* as the leader. If you're the leader, remember that your support is based on respect and trust. Titles identify the one who is to be respected and trusted but they do not create respect and trust. Your gospel-driven life and effective leadership is what creates an environment of respect and trust—so regularly "draw near God, and he will draw near to you" (James 4:8).

Embrace the Team Vision and Mission. It's exciting to see how a church worship team of leaders can help make a vision of genuine God-centered worship into an energized reality when the team embraces the mission with passion, commitment, and humble hearts. Likewise, an outreach team of leaders that embraces its mission will be energized as it accomplishes the mission of planting churches and sending out missionaries. Evidence of spiritual maturity in the life of believers will inevitably energize small group disciple making teams. And on it goes. When a team of leaders embraces the vision and mission, remembering that the vision and the mission must be biblical and thoughtfully contextualized, the team members will inevitably be energized.

Embrace the Members of the Team of Leaders. "And let us consider how to stir up one another to love and good works, not neglecting to meet together, as is the habit of some, but encouraging one another, and all the more as you see the Day drawing near" (Heb. 10:24–25). Team members bring energy to the mission through their interdependent relationships. Even team evaluations, instead of being a source of conflict, can be the catalyst for creating additional energy through the encouragement that comes from a balanced, biblically based evaluation and the mutual desire to stimulate each other to improvement. Remember, if you're the principal leader, you maintain a servant's heart, but don't allow yourself to take over team responsibilities. Don't do what the team can and should do for itself. The team of leaders must own the team leader—and he must own the vision and the mission—and its members must own and support each other. The principal leader should encourage that ownership and support, which will result in energizing both the team and the individual members as they affirm each other's strengths and assist each other in addressing the areas where there is needed improvement.

Embrace Challenges as Opportunities. If a team of leaders has bathed the mission and each other in prayer, then its members will be ready to respond to problems and obstacles as God-given opportunities for growth. The team of leaders must be encouraged to identify problems and obstacles—not deny them. My personal weakness is to deny the presence of problems and obstacles. It is only recently that I have come to understand that they are gifts from a Sovereign God that when faced, solved, and overcome will produce energy and a sense of accomplishment for the team. Team members actually become energized when they work together to solve problems. So, problems are actually an asset to team energy.

Football teams love to play on game day, and they love to score. How do you keep football players focused and engaged in the long hours of practice? The mission is to score, cross the goal line. The coaches create the strategy to accomplish the mission and the players practice all week to implement the strategy knowing that the other team will provide eleven obstacles trying to stop them from scoring. A football team is energized when it comes to practice knowing that it is preparing to effectively remove those eleven obstacles that comprise the opposing team through blocking, running, and passing. The energy to practice as a team is created by the desire to overcome the obstacles in order to implement the strategy or, as it is called today, the game plan, so that the team can score and win the victory. An effective team leader will develop the skills both to encourage team members to accept obstacles and challenges as opportunities and to seek the Lord's solutions. Good leaders should neither deny the existence of problems nor use them as excuses to quit. Again, make prayer a priority and encourage team members to jointly pursue solutions to the problems and obstacles and watch as their energetic engagement grows—and as it grows, the team grows.

The principal leader or team leader can assemble the team, lead it to list the problems, and develop a written strategy to respond. The strategic plan can be divided into tasks and assigned to team members according to their callings, gifts, and talents. Be sure to build in accountability. A prayerful joint effort can energize the team and great blessings can emerge from God-centered problem-solving as the Lord transforms problems into opportunities.

Celebrate the Victories. Whenever God gives a victory, team leaders should pause to celebrate. Appropriate celebration honors the Lord who gave the victory and energizes the team of leaders.

It's a mistake to move right on to the next effort without taking time to celebrate. Every team of leaders—and every leader of a team of leaders—will be blessed by thoughtful celebrations as God's overcoming grace is recognized and the victory of Christ is honored and the team is encouraged.

Remember, you face a powerful adversary. But also remember this: you are not alone. The battle is the Lord's, but you have been called into the battle for the Lord. If in your heart you commit to *defining, developing,* and *deploying* leaders while seeking to be a leader who is faithful, effective, and efficient, Satan will assuredly attack. The last thing that Satan desires is for the church to be committed to becoming a Christian leadership factory and distribution center, reproducing Christian leaders for the church and the world. So what will he do? Thankfully, the Bible has already revealed his assault plan to us. The great heavyweight fighter, Joe Louis, was once asked how he disposed of his opponents so quickly. Reportedly, he replied that he knew them and knew what they were going to do before they knew what they were going to do. You can know what your opponent Satan is going to do before he knows what he is going to do because God's Word tells us what we need to know about our adversary.

15

KNOW YOUR ENEMY

"Submit yourselves therefore to God.
Resist the devil, and he will flee from you."
JAMES 4:7

Satan is defeated. But still he thrashes.

That's the biblical truth. When the God of the ages entered this world wrapped in flesh as Jesus Christ, he was on a threefold mission. His irresistible goals were to save his people from their sins, as proclaimed in Matthew 1:21; to purchase a triumphant church with his own blood, as stated in Ephesians 5:25–27; and to defeat Satan and his works, as asserted in 1 John 3:8. Jesus Christ was victorious over Satan, and the devil's preordained future lies in the lake of fire. But for the present he is still prince of this world, and we Christians are engaged in warfare with him and his allies. Every Christian, especially a leader, needs to know and obey God's directions to put on the "whole armor of God" as directed in Ephesians 6:10–18. By the power of God—not on your own—you *can* thwart the spiritual attack of the enemy and God *can* convert the attack into a victory on your behalf and for his glory.

So it's vital that you know the enemy and what to expect from him. Thankfully, it's all in the Word of God, and by the Spirit of God, through the grace of God we can know it, obey it, and apply it. Let's remember one thing right up front: it's not a battle between gods. Satan is not the bad god and God the good god. There is only one God. Satan is a wannabe—a fallen angel of high rank created by God and now under the judgment of the Sovereign God. Ultimately, in his perfect timing, God will end the days of Satan, to the glory of God and the good of his people. For now, in God's sovereignty, we must remember two essential truths: First, Satan is defeated and is awaiting God's dismissal. As we sing in Martin Luther's great hymn, "A Mighty Fortress Is Our God": "One little word shall fell him." That will occur according to God's timing, not the enemy's. Second, with God as our Protector, we are called to "fight the good fight" (1 Tim. 6:12). Thankfully, we do not have to do it alone as we have been given the Spirit of God and "he who is in you is greater than he who is in the world" (1 John 4:4).

Satan's Strategies

Satan hates what God loves, and that's us, God's people. Satan has two attack strategies: a persecution strategy and a penetration strategy. Satan's persecution strategy is to use *cosmos*—the worldly system of rebellion over which he is prince—to bring persecution against the church of Jesus Christ. He does that by focusing on individual Christian leaders and the church as a whole. It's spiritual warfare, but sometimes he uses evil governments and tyrannical leaders who knowingly or unknowingly follow him. Satan's minions—the evil tyrants of history—never seem to learn what will happen to them for persecuting God's beloved, and ultimately suffer a devastating end as predicted in Psalm 14:4–5: "Have they no knowledge, all the evildoers who eat up my people as they eat bread and do not call upon the LORD? There they [the evildoers] are in great terror, for God is with the generation of the righteous." And by the grace of the Sovereign God, Satan's persecution of believers inevitably becomes an instrument for the growth of the church.

In the book of Acts, for instance, the church was persecuted in Jerusalem, and then multiplied in Judea and Samaria (Acts 7–8). When the atheistic communist regime seized power in China after World War II, there were probably eighty thousand Christians in that nation, and China's communist leaders tried to eliminate them by persecution. Today, there are an estimated 100 million Chinese Christians. Likewise, a series of tyrannical leaders persecuted Christians in Africa, intent on destroying the believers in their despotic regimes. Instead, God sent a revival to East Africa, and the result is a thriving African church with tens of millions of members—including an African Christian leadership now offering spiritual direction to American believers.

Satan's penetration strategy is less obvious than his persecution strategy and more insidious: he seeks to destroy the church from within. It's an old strategy. Paul warned the church at Ephesus about Satan's penetration plan: "I know that after my departure fierce wolves will come in *among you* [the elders of the church], not sparing the flock" (Acts 20:29). Old and exposed as it is, Satan's penetration plan can still do immense damage, often because those under attack don't recognize the assault. It's a two-pronged penetration attack: penetration in the fellowship and penetration in the leadership. When Satan penetrates the fellowship, he will attempt to distract, delay, and eventually destroy the work of the local church through a rising cacophony of complaints and grumbling. And he will also attempt to penetrate the ranks of leaders to discourage and eventually destroy their leadership by placing "fierce wolves"— false teachers—inside the leadership and by luring legitimate leaders into sin. Leaders must resist both attacks by knowing the Word of God, applying it, and calling upon the Lord insistently in prayer.

Beware: Satan targets leaders in particular with his assault strategy. Yet the Bible does not tell the believer or the leader to flee, but to resist Satan and *he* will flee. We're also advised that we should be aware of his assault and allies—his servants, schemes, and snares. According to Scripture, Satan is served by three allies in his rebellion. First are the fallen angels who were cast out of heaven with him under the judgment of God, according to Revelation 12:7–9. While Satan does not have God's omnipresent nature, he is apparently ubiquitous. In other words, he is not everywhere all the time, but he *can* be anywhere at any time. His influence is also expanded by the dispersal of his demonic force of principalities and authorities. While the exact number of demons is unstated in Scripture, it must be significantly large if hundreds can be devoted to one individual as revealed in Mark 5:9.

A second company of allies are the purveyors of the world's system of rebellion against the Lord. Christian leaders must beware of the counterfeit, unholy trinity: the world, the flesh, and the devil. Whenever Satan attacks, he knows he has an ally within the believer—the "flesh" or the "old man," which is the enemy within. He also has allies outside of the believer—"the strongholds of Satan"—composed of institutions promoting worldviews designed to deny the centrality and glory of God.

Satan's third assembly of allies consists of the numerous antichrists who have arisen throughout the ages and litter the pages of history—tyrants who have either intentionally or ignorantly served the purposes of Satan in their lust for power and possessions. John refers to them as the many antichrists that have gone into the world (1 John 2:18), and in 2 Thessalonians 2:3–4 Paul warns of a yet to be revealed major figure who would be called "the" Antichrist. As Satan promotes his schemes and snares through his assault plans and strategies, he is served by all three of his allies—the demonic principalities; the unholy trinity of the world, the flesh, and the devil; and the many antichrists, including political and military tyrants as well as counterfeit religious leaders.

Satan's Schemes

The Bible also teaches that Satan effectively operates three ongoing schemes: "For all that is in the world, the lust of the flesh and the lust of the eyes and boastful pride of life, is not from the Father, but is from the world" (1 John 2:16, NASB). Satan has used, is using, and will continually use these three schemes to attack believers in general and leaders in particular. He uses the lust of the flesh—the addiction of appetites—to draw the tempted away from knowledge of the Holy One. He also uses the lust of the eyes—presenting visual idols to awaken the illicit fulfillment of our appetites. And he uses what Scripture calls the "boastful pride of life" to tempt us into arrogant addictions of valid appetites.

In the garden Adam and Eve were tempted by the lust of the flesh, the lust of the eyes, and the boastful pride of life to disobey God's Word, and they did. Scripture says in Genesis 3:6 that "when the woman saw that the tree was good for food [the lust of the flesh], and that it was a delight to the eyes [the lust of the eyes], and that the tree was to be desired to make one wise [the boastful pride of life], she took from its fruit and she ate. . . ." Satan not only used his threefold schemes on the first Adam, he attempted the same upon the second Adam, Jesus Christ, this time not in a garden but in a wilderness. First Satan unleashed the lust of the flesh, trying to take advantage of Jesus' hunger. "If you are the Son of God," he taunted, "command these stones to become loaves of bread" (Matt. 4:3). Jesus discarded the temptation and responded with the Word of God: "It is written: 'Man shall not live by bread alone, but by every word that comes from the mouth of God'" (Matt. 4:4, quoting Deut. 8:3). He affirmed the sufficiency of God and the priority of the spiritual over the physical—and that's what Christian believers must also do when Satan attacks us with the lust of the flesh. Respond with the Word, and put the spiritual above the physical.

As he continued his futile temptation of the Lord, Satan next appealed to the lust of the eyes, visually offering some of the crown jewels from his temporary domain—what Luke 4:5 refers to as "all the kingdoms of the world." In exchange, the devil asked for what he has really always wanted: "If you, then, will worship me, it will all be yours" (4:7). Setting the model for us, Jesus again dismissed the temptation by quoting the Word: "It is written, 'You shall worship the Lord your God, and him only shall you serve' " (4:8, quoting Deut. 6:13). Remember, when Satan appeals to the lust of the eyes with allurements of power, wealth, or materialism use the Word of God and place the spiritual above the physical, the eternal above the temporal.

In his third and final effort to tempt Jesus, Satan attacked with an appeal to the boastful pride of life, trying to draw Christ into the trap of pride and make him derail his ministry mission in a demonstration of power and influence at the pinnacle of the temple. "If you are the Son of God, throw yourself down from here, for it is written, 'He will command his angels concerning you, to guard you,' and 'On their hands they will bear you up, lest you strike your foot against a stone' " (Luke 4:9–11, quoting Ps. 91:11, 12). Again Jesus replied with the Word of God. "It is written, 'You shall not put the Lord your God to the test.' " His assertion humbly glorified God the Father rather than himself. And Satan fled. Avoid the arrogance of pride you may feel as a leader whether you are challenged or complimented—it's Satan appealing to you with the boastful pride of life.

"The lust of the flesh"—the idolatry of appetites; "the lust of the eyes"—the subtlety of allurements; "the boastful pride of life"—the arrogance of wanting to displace God are the ever present schemes of Satan. Remember, God designs tests so that we will grow. Satan designs temptations to destroy us. At times, Satan will attempt to use God's tests as temptations as he did with Adam and Eve. God had called them to the test of obedience in subduing the earth, ruling the creatures, and being fruitful and multiplying while refraining from eating from the tree of the knowledge of good and evil. Satan turned that test into a temptation. But also know that God can and does use Satan's temptations as his tests in order to grow us as he did with Peter. Peter was tempted by Satan to deny the Lord, but God turned the temptation into a test designed to grow him through broken-ness and the gracious gifts of confession and repentance. So how should we live in light of Satan's strategic allies and schemes?

Flee temptations. Daily kill the "old man." Trust God in the tests of life. Surrender to the power of the Spirit of God. Know and use the Word of God as you put on the armor of God. Stay focused upon the glory of God, with prayerful reliance upon the grace of God as you use the weapons of God to advance the kingdom of God. Finally, remember our Lord's words to his disciples as the evil one came for him through the betrayal of Judas: "Watch and pray that you may not enter into temptation. The spirit is indeed willing, but the flesh is weak" (Matt. 26:41).

Satan's Snares

The three schemes of Satan are usually entwined around the use of his three favorite snares, which are his preferred ploys against Christian leaders. What are they? They're fleshly addictions: addiction to power, addiction to sex, and addiction to money.

Consider the first: addiction to power. Power corrupts. Satan knows that. That's why so many Christian leaders default to controlling people instead of serving people. Beware, leader! You are called to be a servant, not a lord. Which are you? Ask yourself that question early and often, get others who will ask you that question regularly, and always answer that question with judgment-day honesty before the Lord. As a leader, you must establish an ongoing procedure to be sure that you are held accountable to someone in authority over you. And then humbly listen to that person's advice. Practice accountability and submission!

Addiction to sex has always been one of Satan's most powerful weapons (consider all the examples in the Old Testament), but it is now clearly the sin of the age in our culture. Satan also loves to use our culture's preoccupation with illicit sexuality. America is drowning in the cesspool of sexual preoccupation, promiscuity, and perversion—all of which are shamelessly promoted by our mass media. To live oblivious to this is to court disaster. Almost daily, it seems, Christian leaders crumble from this particular ensnarement of Satan. As a Christian leader you must seek accountability from trustworthy colleagues and be open to intentional inquiry by others to assist you in avoiding this snare. One prominent Christian leader managed to stay above reproach in this area for a lifetime of integrity by establishing such safeguards early in his ministry. He never allowed himself to be alone with someone of the opposite sex. Office doors were always left open. His wife or an associate was always present in counseling sessions or meetings with members of the opposite sex. He invited a select group of associates that was always ready to hold him accountable, and he voluntarily placed himself under the authority of a supervisory board of leaders. My advice to every leader is: go thou and do likewise.

Addiction to money is another age-old and always-powerful scheme from Satan's arsenal. The love of money has corrupted or disqualified many ministries and destroyed untold numbers of leaders. There's a reason that the Lord said, "No one can serve two masters, for either he will hate the one and love the other, or he will be devoted to the one and despise the other. You cannot serve God and money" (Matt. 6:24). That's why Proverbs 30:8 proclaims as a prayer: "give me neither poverty nor riches. . . ." You can have little wealth and a meager income and still be addicted to money. A Christian's lifestyle should be arranged to honor the supremacy of Christ and not the "love of money," which is "a root of all kinds of evil" (1 Tim. 6:10). Christian leaders should be accountable to recognized authorities in the area of both personal and ministry financial stewardship. Ministry finances should honor the Lord, and Christian leaders should be transparent and accountable in the area of their financial life. A Christian leader or a ministry should never have cause to be ashamed when financial records are revealed. As one young Christian business leader, who is highly respected in our community, said, "Pastor, in life, the Christian should always do 'the next right thing' for the Lord." Financial conduct demands that sense of integrity from Christian leaders.

Satan's Servants

Christians in general, and leaders in particular, become especially vulnerable to Satan's schemes when affected by one of these servants of Satan: fear, frustration, or fatigue. "The fear of man lays a snare," according to Proverbs 29:25. When we function fearfully, we're susceptible to Satan's lies and deceit. Step back, call on the Lord, plunge into the Word, and turn away from fear. "The Lord is my helper; I will not fear; what can man do to me?" (Heb. 13:6, quoting Ps. 118:6). What's the best defense to fear? It's more than mere personal courage or resolve—it's love. Scripture reveals in 1 John 4:18 that "perfect love casts out all fear." The only perfect love in existence is God's love, and its greatest display is the love of Christ on the cross. "We love because he first loved us" (1 John. 4:19), therefore exercise your love for him by knowing his Word, engaging in prayer, and committing to the biblical priorities of your life and ministry leadership. You cannot personally overcome Satan and his ways of war, but God can easily do it for you in a moment. So look not to yourself, your talents, your gifts, or your self-confidence; in other words, put no confidence in the flesh, it is the spirit who gives life. Therefore call on the Lord and trust fully in the unfailing love of Christ.

Frustration makes us vulnerable to Satan's schemes, and we easily become frustrated when we take on too much. Inspired by the Holy Spirit, Paul declared "one thing I do" (Phil. 3:13). The more our culture embraces complexity, multitasking, and overloading, the more Christian leaders and the church should encourage simplicity in life. Leaders, like others, need margins in life—margins of time for rest and reflection as well as margins in finances for giving and sacrifice. Take charge of simplifying your workload and lifestyle, or engage someone to help you do it. Proverbs 16:9 recognizes that planning is appropriate since we are made in the image of God, but it also reminds us that our planning should be God-centered, and when God redirects our plan we are to respond with contentment and trust: "The heart of a man plans his way, but the LORD establishes his steps."

Rest in the sovereignty of God as he establishes your steps and causes all things to "work together for good, for those who are called according to his purpose" (Rom. 8:28).

Avoid fatigue. It's like a sharpener for Satan's sword. Sometimes fatigue is a legitimate result of being "poured out as a drink offering" (2 Tim. 4:6), but often it's unnecessarily self-imposed. We take on too much. We refuse to say no. We don't listen to advice. We plan poorly, commit quickly, and fail to delegate. We become fatigued. Remember, it is in the multiplication of leaders and the blessing of sharing leadership that much fatigue could be avoided by those who are overwhelmed in leadership.

Those three vulnerabilities—fear, frustration, and fatigue—are often connected. When you become fearful, you don't sleep well, which makes you frustrated, and eventually the two pile on to make you fatigued. Then you're on edge, tense, easily provoked, lacking in judgment, devoid of patience—and you become an enticing target for Satan. Decide now to thwart Satan's use of fear, frustration, and fatigue. Plan for appropriate physical exercise, rest, and regular spiritual renewal. Then you can exercise leadership efficiently—fully functioning physically, mentally, emotionally, and spiritually through a daily trust in the sufficiency of Christ and living out that trust with wisdom and the full use of the means of grace in your life.

Standing Up to Satan

Enjoy the gift of the Sabbath and its benefits. It *is* God's gift to us—even though many believers and leaders fail to fully embrace it. "The Sabbath was made for man, not man for the Sabbath," said the Lord in Mark 2:27. The early Christians made full use of synagogue worship on Saturday for evangelism, but they intentionally turned to assemble as believers for worship on the Lord's Day, commemorating the resurrection of Christ, while maintaining the Sabbath principle—worship and rest one day in seven. Therefore, in the new covenant the apostles by precept and practice set aside the first day of the week, the Lord's Day, as the new covenant Sabbath. Remember, God has made the Sabbath for man and as a blessing to man. So, honor the Sabbath in good conscience. As a Christian leader, my encouragement to others is to use the Lord's Day as it is designed for the Sabbath purpose of physical rest and renewal, time alone with God and with your family, and the gathering of God's people for public worship designed to declare the majesty of our Triune God. The proper use of God's gift of the Sabbath can change your life and provide protection from Satan's allies, strategies, schemes, and servants.

At all times it is absolutely crucial that the Christian leader recognize and remember the victory of Christ over Satan at the cross. Resist Satan, and Scripture promises that he will flee—and do not fear. Remember, your confidence should not be in yourself: it's the Lord who deals with Satan on your behalf. The battle is the Lord's. The Christian leader should embrace the truth of 1 Corinthians 10:31: "So, whether you eat or drink, or whatever you do, do it all to the glory of God." We will not live to eat; we will eat to live for Christ. We will not live to drink; we will drink to live for Christ. Satan tried to defeat Jesus by the lust of the flesh, the lust of the eyes, and the boastful pride of life. Instead, Christ defeated Satan by the Holy Spirit and the Word of God. As Christian leaders, we must know the enemy and deal with him biblically, and remember that Jesus Christ is victorious.

So while you must flee temptation, you must not flee Satan. Instead, as Scripture instructs, resist him: "Submit yourselves therefore to God. Resist the devil, and he will flee from you" (James 4:7). Flee temptation. Resist Satan. Then he will flee from you. Remember these three marvelous gospel truths: First, Jesus defeated Satan and all the principalities and powers of darkness at the cross. Jesus made a mockery of the kingdom of darkness and held it up for ridicule. He has bound the strongman. Granted, God has allowed the devil a lengthy chain for the moment, but he is defeated: "And having disarmed the powers and authorities, [Jesus] made a public spectacle of them, triumphing over them by the cross" (Col. 2:15, NIV). Second, the Bible reveals that the

Holy Spirit lives within you. And the Holy Spirit of God is infinitely greater than Satan who is in the world: "Little children, you are from God and have overcome them, for he who is in you is greater than he who is in the world" (1 John 4:4). Third, Scripture also reveals that Jesus Christ, Lord of lords and King of kings, is continually interceding for you at the throne of God the Father in the magnificent, unfathomable exercise of God's triune glory. Your value to God—the God who will protect you as you resist Satan—is triumphantly proclaimed in Romans 8:33–39:

> Who shall bring any charge against God's elect? It is God who justifies. Who is to condemn? Christ Jesus is the one who died—more than that, who was raised—who is at the right hand of God, who indeed is interceding for us. Who shall separate us from the love of Christ? Shall tribulation, or distress, or persecution, or famine, or nakedness, or danger, or sword? As it is written, "For your sake we are being killed all day long; we are regarded as sheep to be slaughtered." No, in all these things we are more than conquerors through him who loved us. For I am sure that neither death nor life, nor angels nor rulers, nor things present nor things to come, nor powers, nor height nor depth, nor anything else in all creation, will be able to separate us from the love of God in Christ Jesus our Lord.

Christian leader, know the adversary. Know his allies, his strategies, his schemes, his snares, and his servants—and resist him. He will flee from you. Avoid a lifestyle that makes you vulnerable. Do not allow fear, frustration, or fatigue to weaken you but rest in the sufficiency of the preeminence of Christ. We are at war, and in the sovereignty of God, there will be casualties. Some will be wounded. Some will be taken home. Spiritual warfare is a reality of the Christian walk. Stand firm as a leader in the Lord. Lead the way, equipped in the whole armor of God as you "take every thought captive to obey Christ" (2 Cor. 10:5). Be a leader who reproduces and multiplies leaders as you make gospel-driven and Christ-centered disciples. Always make sure that those whom you are discipling are not ignorant of Satan's schemes.

Your marching orders as a Christian leader are plainly stated in 2 Timothy 4:1–5:

> I charge you in the presence of God and of Christ Jesus, who is to judge the living and the dead, and by his appearing and his kingdom: preach the word; be ready in season and out of season; reprove, rebuke, and exhort, with complete patience and teaching. For the time is coming when people will not endure sound teaching, but having itching ears they will accumulate for themselves teachers to suit their own passions, and will turn away from listening to the truth and wander off into myths. As for you, always be sober-minded, endure suffering, do the work of an evangelist, fulfill your ministry.

Define new leaders.
Develop them.
Deploy them.
Reestablish the church as a leadership factory and distribution center. And by God's grace we may hear again, "These men who have turned the world upside down have come here also" (Act 17:6). What glorious days lie ahead and what a glorious opportunity is before us—unleashing Christian leaders who are world-shakers. In actuality these kinds of leaders do not turn the world upside down, but they turn it right side up as the gospel of Jesus Christ is proclaimed and lived in thought, word, and deed. The enemies of God become the people of God. Lives that are in disarray are redeemed, families are reclaimed, and a culture is transformed. O God, do it again and begin with me.

EPILOGUE

My heart's desire is for the church to seize this moment in time. The church might once again become a leadership factory and distribution center. Remember, the church is called "the body of Christ." That means we are body number two for Christ. In body number one, he lived a perfectly righteous life, died an atoning death, rose from the dead, and ascended into heaven where he now intercedes for us. And in that glorified body he will come again. During his ministry in body number one, our Lord was a "leadership factory and distribution center." He modeled Three-D leadership—he *defined*, *developed*, and *deployed* the Three, the Twelve, and the Seventy. The apostles did likewise and produced leaders that "turned the world upside down." Now we, the church, are body number two and must intentionally do as our Savior did in body number one. We must commit to a prioritized strategy of multiplying servant leaders by defining leadership, developing leaders, and deploying servant leaders not only in the church, but for the world.

The church is called a body, a family, and an army—a body displaying unity in the midst of diversity, a family of brothers and sisters in Christ who love their Father, and an army who is at war and in a war. But one thing is clear: the church is not a business. We need leaders who know how to lead diversity into the harmony of mission and redemptive relationships. We need leaders who are fathers and mothers for the Lord's family. And we need combat leaders for the Lord's army. Combat leaders who, like Joshua, are "strong and courageous":

> When Joshua was by Jericho, he lifted up his eyes and looked, and behold, a man was standing before him with his drawn sword in his hand. And Joshua went to him and said to him, "Are you for us, or for our adversaries?" And he said, "No; but I am the commander of the army of the LORD. Now I have come." And Joshua fell on his face to the earth and worshiped and said to him, "What does my lord say to his servant?" And the commander of the LORD's army said to Joshua, "Take off your sandals from your feet, for the place where you are standing is holy." And Joshua did so. (Josh. 5:13–15)

In Joshua's encounter with the captain of the Lord of hosts, which was a christophany, a pre-incarnate appearance of Christ, he learned four vital lessons on leadership:

1. The question for every Christian leader is not, "Is the Lord on my side?" but, "Am I on the Lord's side?"
2. As a Christian leader, I am never first-in-command; at most I am second-in-command, for the Lord is the "Captain."
3. God's battle plan will be foolish to the world, but I should follow his strategy, for "the battle is the Lord's."
4. Christian leadership is ultimately an act of worship: "Take off your sandals from your feet, for the place where you are standing is holy."

Christian leader, make these four lessons the heartbeat of your life and ministry. Rise up. The church for you now waits.

Soli deo Gloria.

> "In the world you will have tribulation. But take heart;
> I have overcome the world" (John 16:33).

NOTES

Chapter 1: God's Model for Leadership
1. C. S. Lewis, *The Weight of Glory and Other Addresses* (San Francisco: HarperSanFrancisco, 2001), 26.

Chapter 4: Defining the Leader
1. Stephen R. Covey, A. Roger Merrill, and Rebecca R. Merrill, *First Things First: To Live, to Love, to Learn, to Leave a Legacy* (New York: Simon & Schuster, 1994), 88–94.

Chapter 6: What *Is* Leadership?
1. *Tear Down This Wall: The Reagan Revolution—A* National Review *History*, compiled by the editors of *National Review* (New York: Continuum, 2004), 35.

2. Harold Moore and Joseph Galloway, *We Were Soldiers Once . . . and Young: The Battle of La Drang, November 14–15, 1965* (Nashville: Flatsigned Press, 1992), 93.

Chapter 7: Thermometer or Thermostat?
1. J. William Jones, *The Life and Letters of Robert Edward Lee: Soldier and Man* (New York: Neale, 1906), 445.

2. Joshua L. Chamberlain to "My Darling Wife," 19 June 1864, Joshua L. Chamberlain Papers, Special Collections, Hawthorne-Longfellow Library, Bowdoin College.

3. Ibid.

Chapter 8: Learning, Living, Leading

1. William J. Johnson, *George Washington the Christian* (New York: Abingdon Press, 1919), 119–20.

Chapter 10: Rancher or Shepherd: Which Are You?

1. See William A. Cohen, *The Art of the Leader* (Englewood Cliffs, NJ: Prentice Hall, 1990).

Chapter 11: Fighting the Good Fight

1. William Seymour, "Journal of the Southern Expedition, 1780–1783," *Pennsylvania Magazine of History and Biography*, 1883, 7:294.

2. John A. Lejeune, *The Reminiscences of a Marine* (Philadelphia: Dorrance and Company, 1930), 383.

Chapter 13: If It Ain't Horse, Carve It Out!

1. One of the books that stimulated my thinking on this is *The Leadership Engine* by Noel Tichy (New York: Harper Business, 1997).

2. C. S. Lewis, *The Problem of Pain* (New York: HarperCollins, 2001), 91.

3. Elizabeth Dodds, *Marriage to a Difficult Man: The Uncommon Union of Jonathan and Sarah Edwards* (Philadelphia: Westminster Press, 1971), 196.

SCRIPTURE INDEX

THE EMBERS TO A FLAME MINISTRY

The Leadership Dynamic was born out of Dr. Harry Reeder's passion for healthy churches because healthy churches must have healthy leaders. Spiritual vitality is a gift that comes from being Christ-centered and gospel-driven through the power of the Holy Spirit. Other than the preaching of God's Word and intercessory prayer, there is no strategy more effective in developing a healthy church and in penetrating the culture for the gospel than the multiplication and distribution of "dynamic leadership."

The ministry Embers to a Flame teaches the paradigm for biblical church health found in Revelation 2:5: "Remember therefore from where you have fallen; repent, and do the works you did at first." Out of the paradigm of Remember, Repent, and Recover, there are ten strategies for church health, one of which is defining, developing, and deploying leaders.

If you would like to explore further the ten strategies of biblical church health, we'd encourage you to prayerfully consider attending an Embers to a Flame conference. These conferences provide an excellent opportunity for a church's leadership to come together and work its way through the biblical principles of church health. During each session of the conference, an experienced church leader teaches a biblical strategy followed by group discussion and practical application.

After the Embers conference, the next step is Fanning the Flame, which partners with a church's leadership to help instill in the life of a church the biblical strategies for church health contained in the Embers conference. During this fourteen-month process, your coach will review with your leadership team the ten strategies taught in the Embers conferences, help make prayer an essential element in the life of your church, administer a church health survey that will identify the greatest area of need for your church, and most importantly, help your leadership instill those habits and skills that lead to a healthy church lifestyle. Your church will also come away with a written vision of what God has called your church to do and be in this generation.

If you are interested in participating in an Embers to a Flame conference or would like more information about Fanning the Flame, please contact us at:

Embers to a Flame
2200 Briarwood Way
Birmingham, AL 35243
205.776.5399
info@emberstoaflame.org
www.emberstoaflame.org